SECRET
BELFAST

D1267849

Kathy Curran and Lorenza Bacino

Gavin Sloan Photography
with contributions from Hunter Bros, Belfast

JONGLEZ PUBLISHING

travel guides

Dr **Kathy Curran** grew up in South Belfast and later studied common and civil law (with French) at Queen's University Belfast. She then headed to England to pursue a Masters and Doctorate in criminology at the University

of Cambridge. As a criminologist, she loves unearthing gritty stories and tales; a successful combination with her fondness for exploration and travel. She is happiest pottering around ancient graveyards and former prisons and always tries to fit in a trip to a crime museum when on holiday.

Lorenza Bacino is a freelance journalist and travel writer. She is a former radio broadcaster and has also worked as a language teacher, translator and editor. She is usually busy thinking about where to travel to next. Interests and hobbies include

books, film and art. Her family would say she needs to improve her cooking skills – Lorenza tends to agree.

We have taken great pleasure in drawing up *Secret Belfast* and hope that through its guidance you will, like us, continue to discover unusual, hidden or little-known aspects of the city.

Descriptions of certain places are accompanied by thematic sections highlighting historical details or anecdotes as an aid to understanding the city in all its complexity.

Secret Belfast also draws attention to the multitude of details found in places that we may pass every day without noticing. These are an invitation to look more closely at the urban landscape and, more generally, a means of seeing our own city with the curiosity and attention that we often display while travelling elsewhere…

Comments on this guidebook and its contents, as well as information on places we may not have mentioned, are more than welcome and will enrich future editions.

Don't hesitate to contact us:
E-mail: info@jonglezpublishing.com
Jonglez Publishing
25 rue du Maréchal Foch
78000 Versailles, France

NORTH

CHANNEL

Glenarm

Ballygally

Larne

p. 124

Ballyclare

Carrickfergus

Belfast Lough

M2

A8(M)

B95

Newtownabbey

Bangor

M5

Holywood

Donaghad

M2

M3

Dundonald

Newtownards

BELFAST

p. 8

Moneyreagh

Comber

Greyabbey

M1

Strangford

Carryduff

Lough

N

Ballygowan

Kircub

Saintfield

0   5 km   10 km

p. 90

CONTENTS

City Centre

South of the City

North of the City

City Centre

ART DECO ELEPHANT SCULPTURES

A fine example of Indian-inspired Art Deco architecture

Burton building, Ann Street, BT2 7HR
Buses: 1, 1a, 1b, 1c

alfway down Ann Street, at the junction with Telfair Street, cast your gaze upwards and to the left: you will see two sizeable geometric elephants carved out of pale Portland stone on top of the columns on the facade of a three-storey building.

Designed by Harry Wilson of Leeds between 1931 and 1933, this building used to belong to Burton's, the fashion retailer, which began selling men's readymade suits just after 1900.

A Lithuanian-born Jew, Sir Montague Maurice Burton began his career in the UK as a peddler, but by the time he died in 1952, he had the largest tailoring empire of its kind in the world.

Burton used architecture for branding purposes and adopted Art Deco as the in-house style for many of his stores across Northern Ireland. He employed classic geometric stylised patterns as well as the Indian- and Egyptian-inspired elephants so beloved by the Art Deco movement in the 1920s and 30s. The elephants, whose tusks are pointing in different directions, were designed by E.A. Moore.

Few of Burton's buildings had such ornate decoration, making the Belfast store one of the finest surviving examples of the iconic Burton brand. Unfortunately, it is now a little dilapidated.

Elephants can also be spotted inside Belfast's splendid Grand Opera House, located on Great Victoria Street. Opened in 1895, it was designed by theatre architect Frank Matcham, who is also responsible for many British theatres, including the London Palladium and the London Coliseum. The Theatres Trust considers the interior of the Grand Opera House to be one of the best surviving examples of oriental-style theatre architecture in the UK. The plush gold and red interior is adorned with intricate Indian-inspired detail, particularly on the curved fronts of the two balconies. The ceiling is divided into ornate painted panels. The large gilded elephant heads are easy to spot at the front of the auditorium.

Art Deco

The term "Art Deco" comes from the Exposition Internationale des Art Décoratifs et Industriels Modernes, held in Paris in 1925. Emerging as a recognisable style in the inter-war years of the 20th century, Art Deco embraced new technologies and discoveries – most significantly, a new form of architecture, distinguished by its geometric shapes inspired by modern art movements such as Cubism. Ancient civilisations such as the Egyptians, Mayans and Aztecs provided other sources of inspiration.

JAFFE MEMORIAL DRINKING FOUNTAIN

②

An ode to Belfast's Jewish community

Victoria Square, BT1 4QG
Buses: 18, 19, 26, 26a, 26b, 27, 28, 31

The Jaffe Memorial Drinking Fountain hasn't always been at its present location at the entrance to the Victoria Street Shopping Centre, although that's where it was originally placed in 1874. Sir Otto Jaffe, Belfast's one and only Jewish mayor, erected it to commemorate his father Daniel Jaffe, a linen merchant and founder of the city's first synagogue in Great Victoria Street.

In fact, this gilded, cast-iron Victorian water feature spent 70 years neglected and ignored in the Botanic Gardens in the south of the city. It was moved there in 1933 and was only returned to its original spot in 2008, following extensive and painstaking restoration in England, in order to mark the opening of the shopping centre. It was in such a fragile state upon arrival that it had to be taken apart piece by piece before it could be restored and regilded to its original form and colour.

The fountain symbolises an important link in Belfast's colourful history, as the Jewish community is one of Northern Ireland's oldest ethnic and religious minorities. The community has only about 80 members today, but punches well above its weight in terms of contributing to the city's cultural and religious life.

Jews first arrived in Belfast back in the 1860s and were mainly active in the linen trade. Daniel Jaffe arrived from Germany for just that reason in 1850. One of nine children, his son Otto went on to become Lord Mayor in 1899 and again in 1904. He established the Jaffe Public Elementary School in 1907 – it was open to both Protestant and Catholic children. At various times throughout his time in Belfast, Jaffe experienced anti-Jewish sentiment. The most notable incident occurred when a group of Belfast women refused to support the Children's Hospital as long as Sir Otto and his wife remained on its board.

NEARBY
The portraits of Bittles Bar

Right beside the Jaffe Fountain is Bittles Bar, a small Victorian-era bar in a flat-iron shape. Despite its size, the bar holds a remarkable selection of beers and whiskeys. While you're sipping on its fare, sit back and take in the eclectic art that adorns the walls. The portraits mainly celebrate Ireland's literary and sporting heroes but also convey some of the gossip that surrounds several of Northern Ireland's more well-known politicians.

CARVED HEADS ON THE ROBINSON & CLEAVER BUILDING

The missing head from a forgotten department store

1-3 Donegall Square N, BT1 5GA
Buses: 12a, 12b, 12c, 12d

Carved from Northern Irish Scrabo sandstone and red Scottish granite, the Robinson & Cleaver building boasts a wonderful collection of 50 carved heads as a tribute to the store, its patrons, its international reputation and achievements.

They include Queen Victoria and Prince Albert, General Washington, the then Prince and Princess of Wales, and the Emperor and Empress of Germany.

Other heads represent countries to where R&C sent out its goods – Canada, Scotland and Australia, as symbolised by a beautiful female head emerging from a veil. The head representing Canada was posed for by Lady Dufferin, whose family seat was the Clandeboye Estate in County Down.

If you look carefully at the heads along the ground floor, you'll notice that one is missing (just above what is now Burger King): it marks the place where the head of the Dowager Empress of Germany (mother of Kaiser Wilhelm II and eldest daughter of Queen Victoria) used to be. During the First World War, an angry mob gathered one night, hacked off her head and smashed it onto the ground below in a show of animosity towards Germany.

Designed by local architects Young & MacKenzie, Robinson & Cleaver opened in 1874, selling tweed and Irish linen at a time when great changes were underway in the city as a result of an economic boom. With the growth of the linen industry came other industries: rope-making and shipbuilding. In the 19th century, Belfast's population expanded exponentially from 20,000 to 350,000.

An affluent class began to emerge: its members wanted to buy beautiful things for their homes, not least to show off their new-found wealth.

Robinson & Cleaver served that need and became the "go-to" store at this time, both for the women of the household and their servants. As such, it became a very female-centric place.

For the first time in Belfast, women had a place to meet and to shop and somewhere men rarely set foot.

It gave them an element of economic power and therefore a degree of independence for the first time. R&C was considered a very prestigious place to work and the store was extremely choosy about who it employed. Seamstresses and cashiers were carefully vetted.

The store became famous for its seasonal window displays, especially at Christmas time.

John Cleaver himself once lived in a mansion on the Malone Road in Belfast. You can see the remnant of his home in the form of a crumbling pillar on the corner of Cleaver Avenue.
For walking tours of Belfast that highlight little-known and forgotten buildings, contact PLACE, 7–9 Lower Garfield Street, BT1 1FP. Tel: 028 90 232524.

FAMINE WINDOW (4)

A glorious window depicting heart-breaking scenes from the Irish famine

City Hall, Donegall Square, BT1 5GS
028 90 320202
www.belfastcity.gov.uk
Mon–Fri 8.30am–5pm, Sat and Sun 10am–4pm, subject to change
Free public tours are available daily, check website for details
Buses: 1, 1a, 1b, 1c, 1d

Visitors to City Hall often miss the window known as the "famine window" as it is not presently included in the official tour. To find it, look for the fourth window along the east corridor on the left side as you enter through the front doors. With its array of vibrant, modern colours, this striking window depicts one of the greatest horrors that ever plagued Ireland. Called in Gaelic "*an Gorta Mór*" (the Great Hunger) or "*an Drochshaol*" (the bad life), this famine plagued Belfast from the mid-1840s. One of the more moving images in the window is that of a woman in a graveyard and a destitute father and daughter weeping over a pot. Elsewhere, a woman and a child toil in a field searching for edible potatoes amid the blight-ravaged crops. In the lower middle section of the window is Clifton House (see below), a building located in the centre of Belfast that was once used as the poor house. A crouched female figure grieving by gravestones in the top right corner was an all too familiar sight in a tragedy that affected everyone, irrespective of social status. Also depicted in the window is the blessed escape of the emigrant ship, at least for those who could afford the cost of a ticket to the New World. America is shown bathed in golden sunlight, representing hope for anyone who was able to reach its shores. This window is part of a series of stained-glass windows throughout the City Hall. It reflects the significant impact that the traumatic famine years have had on Irish consciousness and on the city of Belfast itself. Many Irish historians believe that the word "famine" is itself a misnomer, as the country was in fact producing enough crops at the time, but other factors such as land acquisitions, absent landlords and the punitive 1690 penal laws effectively caused the death of millions.

Straining already frayed relations between the Irish and the British Crown, the famine is considered a watershed in the Irish historical narrative. Indeed, many modern historians refer to the preceding period of Irish history as "pre-famine". One million people are known to have died as a result of it. Another million escaped by emigrating. Those who died from starvation were buried in mass common graves in the Shankill, Friar's Bush, Clifton Street and Donegall Road graveyards across the city. The graveyard of Friar's Bush has a "cholera pit" and is probably the most famous.

Visitors interested in the plight of the Irish poor may like to visit the former poor house, Clifton House, a short walk from the City Hall in North Queen Street. Established in 1774 by the Belfast Charitable Society as a base for their work with the destitute, it is one of the finest examples of Georgian architecture in the city. Both group and individual guided tours of Clifton House are available by phoning ahead to arrange a time or by emailing: lucy@cliftonbelfast.org.uk (see p. 56).

SEAMAN MAGENNIS MEMORIALS ⑤

Memorial to a brave, working-class soldier

Belfast City Hall, Donegall Square South, BT1 5GS
028 90 320202
Mon–Fri 8.30am–5pm, Sat and Sun 10am–4pm (subject to change)
Grounds: Mon–Sun 9.30am–7pm
Buses: 1a, 1b, 1c, 1d, 1e, 1f, 1g

While you're strolling around Belfast's magnificent City Hall Gardens, admiring the statues on display within the grounds, take a moment to examine the circular bronze and Portland stone memorial that stands next to the large statue of Queen Victoria. It was erected in 1999 to commemorate the bravery of James Joseph Magennis (1919–86), a working-class Catholic from the Falls Road.

Magennis is Northern Ireland's only recipient of the Victoria Cross, the highest award in the United Kingdom honours system, awarded for gallantry to members of the British armed forces. However, it took the city half a century to honour him. Magennis served as a diver in His Majesty's Midget Submarine XE-3 in Singapore during the 31 July 1945 attack on a Japanese cruiser, the *Takao* (codenamed Operation Struggle). He worked for an exhausting 45 minutes, with damaged breathing apparatus, to attach limpet mines onto the hull of the cruiser to try and disable it. Despite fatigue and cuts all over his hands, Magennis then volunteered to return to the depths in order to free a jammed carrier. After seven minutes of nerve-wracking labour, he succeeded in releasing it. He received the Victoria Cross for displaying courage and disregard for his own safety.

As City Hall tour guide Christopher Burns explains, "It would have been expected at the time that he receive the honour of the Freedom of the City, but he did not, maybe as much due to his social class as his faith. As a working-class Catholic, it is arguable that his achievements were to a certain extent overlooked by the establishment, and as a British soldier it appears he was again overlooked by his own community."

A long campaign by his biographer resulted in a re-evaluation of Magennis' actions and the erection of this memorial. The bronze frieze around the top of the statue recreates the scene surrounding the events in 1945, as told to the artist Elizabeth McLaughlin by Magennis himself shortly before his death.

Mural of Magennis in Tullycarnet

Opposite Melfort Drive in Tullycarnet, Belfast, a mural depicting Magennis is a poignant reminder that his bravery is now recognised by both sides of the religious divide in Northern Ireland. It was commissioned for the 60th anniversary of VJ (Victory in Japan) Day in 2005 by Peter Robinson, a prominent unionist (Protestant) politician.

"TROUBLED IMAGES" EXHIBITION ⑥

A vibrant and striking collection of political posters

Linen Hall Library, 17 Donegall Square N, BT1 5GB
028 90 321707
www.linenhall.com
Mon–Fri 9.30am–5.30pm, Sat 9.30am–4pm
Free

Entering the Linen Hall Library via the side entrance on Fountain Street allows access to the "Troubled Images" exhibition, a collection of 70 thought-provoking and iconic posters that line the walls of the vertical gallery of this famous library and are well worth closer examination.

Those on show, selected from over 3,000 posters held in the library's renowned Northern Ireland Political Collection, are significant in terms of their historical importance and sheer artistry. The posters tell the history of Belfast's political conflict and subsequent peace process from the early 1970s to the late 1990s. They depict the genesis of campaigns and protests fought by the families of victims of violence, exploited workers or those who were trying to protect their community from threat.

There are posters inciting political protest, memorialising the dead and pleading for an end to violence, with civil and religious liberties for all. One of the most famous peace movements in Northern Ireland was started by the Peace People, one of whose early posters is featured here. Its founders were women (one of whom had lost three nieces and nephews). The posters spell out their plea, "STOP THE WAR!", and were seen at peace rallies across the province and involving all communities. This was a significant achievement and its founders were awarded the Nobel Peace Prize in 1977.

Among the posters that depict the animosity between religious groups over the years, a dark humour emerges. For example, with the summer Protestant marching season beginning, one poster depicts the Pope with his head in his hands under the title, "Oh NO! Not Drumcree again." If you look closely, the Pope has the figure 666 (symbol of the devil) emblazoned on his orange sash.

Since its launch in 2001, this unique exhibition has travelled to the United States, the Basque country, and Gaza and the West Bank. The library sells a CD-Rom featuring the majority of posters held in the Northern Ireland Political Collection.

NEARBY

Round the corner from the library in College Street, on the piazza at the Fountain Shopping Centre, is the only automaton clock in Ireland. The Alice Clock was created in the year 2000 to celebrate the Millennium. Between 9am and 6pm, 24 bells play on the hour, each hour. Characters from Lewis Carroll's *Alice in Wonderland* rotate around the three mosaic panels and represent morning, noon and night.

AL-HIDAYA PLAQUE

A great interpretation of Islamic law by a Belfast man

Rosemary Street Presbyterian Church, 41 Rosemary Street, BT1 1QB
www.nspresbyterian.org
028 92 290037
Open most afternoons
Free
Buses: 1, 1a, 1c, 1d, 1e, 1f, 1g, 1j

The vestibule of a Presbyterian church is not where you would expect to see a commemoration of an important document about Islamic law. However, the Rosemary Street Presbyterian Church proudly boasts a plaque shaped like an urn that would have housed a special commentary on Islamic law called *Al-Hidaya* ("the guidance").

The plaque was placed here by the sisters of Charles Hamilton in recognition of his work as the translator of a commentary on Islamic law in the 1780s. It is over 200 years since he translated the text, yet it was only updated about a decade ago.

Charles Hamilton was born in Belfast circa 1752 and, after studying oriental languages, became a talented translator and passionate orientalist. He joined the East India Company and in 1776 travelled to India, where he was promoted to the rank of lieutenant two years later. While in India, Hamilton experienced active service against the Rohillas, who had settled in northern India from Afghanistan. As a lover of local languages, he wrote a history of this Afghan tribe by studying original native texts and other documents. His work was published in London in 1787. He subsequently became one of the first members of the Asiatic Society of Calcutta.

Such was the importance of *Al-Hidaya* that Hamilton was granted a five year leave of absence to complete his translation. Written in Arabic in the 12th century by an Islamic jurist called Burhan al-Din al-Marghinani, the document was considered vital to Britain's running of India's legal administration during the time of Empire (see below). The original text was translated into Persian in the late 18th century – this is the version used by Hamilton for his interpretation, which was published in London in 1791. Hamilton died of tuberculosis aged 39 in 1792, before he could return to his beloved India.

Al-Hidaya played an influential role during Britain's colonisation of South Asia. Islamic and British law were merged as a result of the translation to create what became known as Anglo-Muhammadan law. The text was used by British judges in the colonies to adjudicate in the name of sharia. The document limited the influence of the muftis within the sharia system as it eliminated the need for them to act as middlemen between Islamic law and the colonial administration.

PEW 33 INSIDE ROSEMARY STREET ⑧ FIRST PRESBYTERIAN CHURCH

Belfast's unknown anti-slavery hero and campaigner

41 Rosemary Street, BT1 1QB
www.nspresbyterian.org
028 92 290037
Most afternoons (best to call ahead)
Buses: 1, 1a, 1c, 1d, 1e, 1f, 1g, 1j

Pew 33 inside Rosemary Street First Presbyterian Church is marked with a spoof newspaper headline which reads, "Belfast 1786, McCabe thwarts proposal to set up a slave ship company in Belfast". Few in Belfast have ever heard of Thomas McCabe, who was instrumental in preventing the expansion of the slave trade to Northern Ireland in the 18th century. He was a member of the First Presbyterian Church and sat in Pew 33 when he attended services here. According to Belfast historian Raymond O'Regan, McCabe (who was a watchmaker and jeweller) specifically deserves recognition because of his actions in 1786. A group of wealthy merchants were planning to buy a ship to transport goods from Belfast to Africa's Gold Coast (now Ghana), capture slaves and take them on to the West Indies. Bringing products such as sugar, cotton and tobacco to England and Ireland was a lucrative business, with one round trip reputedly worth up to £20,000. McCabe stepped in to prevent this. When attending the planning meeting, he stood up and shouted, "May God wither the hand who gives the first guinea." McCabe's intervention ensured that this initiative was thwarted, although the slave trade was not abolished

throughout the colonies until 1834. Poignantly, in 2007, some two centuries later, William Wilberforce's great-great-grandson, also named William, came to the church to acknowledge McCabe's brave stance. He brought a black casket made from the iron ankle shackles of slaves. It had been presented to his great-great-grandfather by slaves in recognition of all he had done to push anti-slavery legislation through parliament.

The portrait that can be seen in what is known as the church's "session room" is of the first Minister, Reverend McBride. Bizarrely, it has a hole in it. This is because as, a Presbyterian, he was frequently persecuted by Anglican soldiers who, on one occasion, made it as far as his bedroom. McBride had already escaped, so, in a fit of rage, the soldiers slashed his portrait instead.

ROYAL ULSTER RIFLES MUSEUM

Blood-stained letter from the Battle of the Somme

5 Waring Street, BT1 2EW
(Behind the black steel railings at the back of the Old War Memorial Building)
028 90 232086
www.royal-irish.com
Tues–Fri 10am–4pm (or by appointment)
Free
Buses: 1,1a, 1c, 1d, 1e, 1f, 1g, 1j

Hidden behind a bustling Belfast street, the one-room Royal Ulster Rifles Museum retains some extraordinary items displayed in the fashion of a private collection.

Brimming with war artefacts of "The Regiment", the museum relates to the exploits of The Royal Irish Rifles, a regiment that served with great distinction throughout many conflicts from its beginnings in 1793 during the reign of George III to its involvement in the Indian Mutiny of 1857–58 and the Boer War of 1881.

Three Victoria Crosses were won by soldiers in The Rifles at the 1916 Battle of the Somme.

In 1921 the name was changed to The Royal Ulster Rifles 83rd & 86th. Both battalions took part in the D-Day landings and served in the 1950–53 Korean War.

Items housed here include original bicycles from the D-Day landings, the entrance keys to Colditz Castle and priceless flags, or "colours", dating back to 1810.

Of particular note, among the numerous glass cabinets, is a blood-splattered, handwritten letter that was given to a young officer, Lieutenant Harry Dolling.

This young man had the unenviable task of burying the dead at the Battle of the Somme on 1 July 1916.

The instructions have clearly been scribbled in haste, but there is a helpful accompanying transcription.

The note begins: "Removal of all wounded and burial of all dead in Thiepval Wood and No Man's Land belonging to 36th division. Identity discs and all papers belonging to our dead are to be carefully collected and sent to Div Hdqtrs. Dead to be buried in shell holes or special trench ..."

The note goes on to remind Dolling to apply quicklime freely to help dispose of the bodies. It is thought that he took three days to complete these awful duties. According to his widow, Hazel Dolling, who donated the items to the museum, "The horror [of those days] remained with him all his life." Mrs Dolling uncovered the burial orders' letter after her husband died, in an envelope marked: "This is worth keeping".

The piece of paper, along with pictures and booklets about Dolling, are on display at the museum.

Friendly curator Gavin Glass can explain to visitors how the museum came to own each item and often has ongoing communication with the donor families.

HIDDEN ARTEFACTS
IN THE MERCHANT HOTEL

Ceramic eggs and a mechanical music box are
among the treasures in Belfast's most luxurious hotel

16 Skipper Street, BT1 2DZ
(In the Cathedral Quarter on the corner of Skipper Street and Waring Street)
028 90 234888
www.themerchanthotel.com

Well known for its Italianate exterior of Giffnock sandstone, luxurious furnishings and the fact that the building was once the headquarters of the Ulster Bank, the Merchant Hotel contains several ancient and hidden artefacts unearthed during the hotel's £16.5 million extension in 2010. During the second phase of refurbishment, builders dug deep to create a lower ground floor spa as the Merchant is located in one of the oldest parts of the city: the construction team had to work alongside the archaeologists who oversaw the excavations.

One of the most astonishing finds was a large piece of a jug or bowl painted with the date 1676. This currently resides with the team of archaeologists who completed the original dig.

A more peculiar find was a set of small ceramic eggs, now known as the "entrance eggs", which grace the exterior lobby. The team of archaeologists found 30 eggs in total: a small number are now on display in a horizontal cabinet at the front entrance to the hotel. It is thought that these replica "dummy eggs" were placed in hen houses to either encour-

age or discourage nesting. These particular eggs may have belonged to a private householder centuries ago. However, as the hotel is in the historic mercantile heart of Belfast, it is also possible they may have had some commercial use. Elsewhere in the hotel, the Great Room Restaurant boasts breathtaking architecture, which could make it easy to miss the polyphon in the corner: in this mechanical music box, the tune is punched out on the disc with pitch determined by the position of the holes. Although made in Germany, this particular item was purchased from André Bissonnet's quaint old-instrument shop on Rue Du Pas de la Mule in Paris. One of the joys of visiting the Merchant Hotel lies in discovering what other quirky gems hide in its secluded corners. Everything seems to have a story behind it. Even the residents' billiard room was once a former safe.

NEARBY

At the junction of Waring Street, Donegall Street, North Street and Bridge Street, the oldest part of the city – known colloquially as "the Four Corners" – is the place from which all milestones from Belfast were once measured. Diagonally opposite the Merchant Hotel, Sugarhouse Entry is where the United Irishmen met in Peggy Barclay's Tavern. They were an 18th-century political group that aimed to remove Irish affairs from English control. Belfast was known then as the "Boston of the North" because of the actions of radical Presbyterians, who, as members of the United Irishmen, attempted to unite Catholics, Protestants and Dissenters.

KING BILLY'S CHAIR

*King William of Orange's chair is still in use
in a corner of the church*

St George's Church, 105 High Street, BT1 2AG
028 90 231275
www.stgeorges.connor.anglican.org
Weekdays 10am–3pm, Sat 10am–1pm
Buses: 1, 1a, 1b, 1c, 1d

To the left of the altar in St George's Church, a small chair usually stands strangely isolated: it was used by Prince William III of Orange, known locally as "King Billy", who stopped here in 1690 on his way from Carrickfergus to the Battle of the Boyne, and is sometimes called "King Billy's Chair" by those in the know. It's rather on the small side as King Billy was only a metre and a half tall (he is usually painted on horseback to conceal his diminutive stature).

King Billy spent a week in Belfast and sat in this chair while attending a Sunday service. Visitors are free to sit where William of Orange sat all those centuries ago.

St George's is the oldest Anglican Church of Ireland in the city and is renowned for its traditions of music and inclusiveness. In the 1650s, Oliver Cromwell's troops stole lead from the roof to make musket balls while attempting to impose a republic upon Ireland. It used to be possible to sail along the River Farset right up to the church doorway and the Farset still runs in a tunnel beneath the High Street. The street opposite St George's is called Skipper Street and is where seamen could find lodgings while on dry land.

NEARBY

Three enormous buoys are on display as public works of art in Cathedral Gardens adjacent to St Anne's Cathedral. The buoys are of the type used in local waters and were mistakenly painted using incorrect colours, which has caused quite a stir in the maritime community. Belfast Harbourmaster Captain Kevin Allen says, "The round buoy indicates a safe water mark and should be red and white. The other conical-shaped buoy should be green, according to modern conventions, and the can-shaped buoy should be painted red."

More than 50 years old, the buoys were donated to the council by the Commissioner of Irish Lights in the 1980s in recognition of the city's maritime legacy. Belfast City Council has promised to rectify the mistake the next time the buoys are repainted.

A bronze statue of Northern Ireland's favourite boxer, John Joseph Monaghan (1918–84), better known as "Rinty", stands in the gardens, looking out across his home town. Rinty was world flyweight boxing champion in 1948 and, as such, was the first boxer from the city to win a world title. He is shown holding a microphone as he used to burst into a rendition of *When Irish Eyes are Smiling* at the end of his fights. He is a local hero and inspired many others to follow in his footsteps.

MURIEL'S CAFÉ BAR

Hidden gin palace in the Cathedral Quarter

12–14 Church Lane, BT1 4QN
028 90 332445
Daily 10am–12am

Muriel's Café Bar has a fairly unassuming and modern exterior, but don't let this mislead you. Step inside this Grade II listed building and you're immediately struck by its "intimate" feel, spelled out across the ceiling in the form of "lingerie bunting". Pants, bras and other garish garments hang like washing from the walls.

The burlesque-like interior hints at the building's naughty past, when sailors would frequent the brothel upstairs, while downstairs Muriel the Milliner produced hats for the good people of Belfast. Muriel is thought to have resided here some 150 years ago, when her more clandestine business benefited from its proximity to the River Lagan and a regular flow of clientele from passing ships. Although Muriel's is no longer a brothel, it does offer a heady array of gins (167 varieties). As bar supervisor John Shields says, "Gin is our thing." Those who work at Muriel's are not only admired for their knowledge but for their capacity for experimentation. They will try anything with gin: mango, cardamom, rosemary … you name it. Arguably the most unique and highly valued concoction from Muriel's menu is known as the Jawbox, a wonderful local gin garnished here with home-made honeycomb, lime and ginger ale. Its name harks back to the time when houses in this part of world did not have indoor sinks. People did their washing communally around a large sink known as a "jawbox", which became the place for a good gossip. Jawbox gin is made locally at the Echlinvelly distillery, Northern Ireland's first licensed distillery in over 125 years. Muriel's is an inclusive joint that values regulars from all backgrounds. Upstairs, Bohemian artists mix with suits in a bar that resembles a New York speakeasy, with just a touch of Vegas thrown in. The more adventurous gin-lover can join the Juniper Club. Members get to "travel" around the world in 80 gins by reaching into a proffered suitcase, retrieving a prize and trying out the particular gin inscribed on the luggage tag.

CARVED HEADS ON MARLBOROUGH STREET

Victorian values depicted in carved stone heads

Marlborough Street, BT1
Buses: 1, 1a, 1b, 1c

A rather lovely and unusual head can be seen on Marlborough Street at the keystone of one of the two visible archways on this narrow and unassuming street. Look up to see the small head of a Chinese gentlemen with a plait, wearing a conical hat and sporting a downturned curly moustache. The head from the other archway is missing, but artist and historian Daniel Jewesbury managed to locate it in a heritage store just outside town. It is the head of an African male with beautifully carved hair and a broken chain around the neck: a symbol of Belfast's anti-slavery stance.

These heads are the work of architectural sculptors Thomas, William and Michael Fitzpatrick and a number of them adorn the facades of several 19th-century buildings in the centre of town.

Other beautiful examples can be seen on the office building dating from the 1860s at No. 55–59 Donegall Street, the former location of the old *Belfast News Letter*. There are eight heads on the front that were previously unidentified. However, Jewesbury says that at the time of opening in 1737, the *News Letter* listed them as Henry Cooke, the firebrand Presbyterian preacher; the Governor General of Ireland, the Duke of Abercorn; and the 14th Earl of Derby, Edward Smith Stanley, a three-time Tory politician who was responsible for introducing the Irish education system into the country. Their presence here reflects the conservatism of the *Belfast News Letter,* which is the oldest English-language newspaper in Ireland and still in print today. The Fitzpatricks used their artistry to reflect values such as unionism, conservatism and freedom of the press in the very fabric of the city.

The Fitzpatrick brothers were responsible for changing the face of new buildings in Belfast between the late 1850s and the 1890s; they found their inspiration in Italianate, neo-Renaissance and neo-Venetian sculpture. Most of their "roundels", as they're known in the architectural jargon, represent famous people of the time, as well as mythical and symbolic themes. Jewesbury has managed to identify a significant number of them around town, but explains that because the brothers were first and foremost builders, information on their architectural achievements is hard to come by.

More examples of fine Fitzpatrick heads

The Malmaison Hotel (34–38 Victoria Street), a former warehouse, boasts five tall pilasters representing the five continents, topped with carvings of agricultural produce and stylised heads. These were carved by the youngest Fitzpatrick brother, Michael, who died at the age of 32. The rest of the facade is decorated with a host of other carvings and sculptures, again reflecting Victorian values of Empire, civilisation, progress, science and culture.

CALDER FOUNTAIN

The grandest horse trough in the city

Custom House Square, BT1 3ET
Buses: 1a, 1b, 1c, 1d, 1e, 1f, 1g, 1j

In Victorian times, a number of water troughs were strategically placed throughout the city so that working horses could quench their thirst. The majestic sandstone fountain at the southern fringe of the revamped

Custom House Square, diagonally opposite McHughs (the oldest pub in Belfast), is particularly grand. It was erected to commemorate Commander Francis Anderson Calder, who did so much to prevent cruelty to horses and other animals.

In the 19th century, Belfast was a loud, bustling, dirty place, teeming with horse-drawn carriages, its streets echoing to the clip-clop of hooves over cobbles. The city's market traders would have been lost without their horses. In fact, it was thanks to these beasts of burden that Belfast developed so quickly. However, they were not always treated with the respect they deserved. Calder was a pious man with a soft spot for these creatures. Popular blood sports of the era, such as cock-fighting and bear-baiting, further fuelled his sense of outrage and led him, with a group of highly respected citizens and clergymen, to found the BSPCA (Belfast Society for the Protection and Care of Animals) in 1936. It made history as the first organisation to fight for animal rights and soon became renowned throughout the British Isles, in particular for setting up water troughs for Belfast's horses and cattle. Between the years 1843 and 1855, 10 such troughs were installed, including one on Oxford Street. This horse trough was originally placed in 1859 in Queen's Square, where it received little attention or care. For many years it lay open to the elements, crumbling beneath the tide of passing time and history. In August 2003 the Laganside Corporation decided to revive it and sought the help of stone restoration experts, S McConnell & Sons. Today it stands revitalised near its original location in Custom House Square, the epicentre of 19th-century Belfast.

The Calder Fountain is one of the few horse troughs (out of the original 21) still standing and is the most majestic. The troughs were dotted about town, including the one on Oxford Street (see historic picture).

NEARBY

Just opposite the Calder Fountain is McHughs Bar, which is more than 300 years old. It was built at a time when the River Farset ran the whole way down the high street from the original location of Belfast Castle. While not visible today, the river still runs underneath High Street and Queen's Square.

BELFAST'S SEAL COLONY

Boat tours take you to see Belfast's thriving seal colony

Musgrave Channel, off Donegall Quay
Lagan Boat Company, The Obel, 66 Donegall Quay, BT1 3NG
028 90 240124/ 07718 910 423
www.laganboatcompany.com
Open all year round

Although most people in Belfast are unaware of this, a handful of common seals were spotted in the Musgrave Channel five years ago. Now the colony numbers over 75, mostly mothers and babies: it is accessible to boats from Donegall Quay that have been granted special permission.

A protected species, the common seal is particularly attractive with its "puppy-dog" face. The best time to spot the seals is at low tide, which varies by an hour each day.

Derek Booker OBE, of the Lagan Boat Company, has been taking people out in his boat for over 15 years. He is hugely knowledgeable about Belfast's maritime history and knows the finest places to spot

River Lagan's wildlife. Summer provides the best opportunity for seal spotting as the seals will have quitted the harbour and followed the fish out to sea by the end of October.

Booker explains that the seals came here largely because the river was cleaned and fish began to return.

The cleaner environment also attracted many other types of fish and lots of birdlife, including black guillemots.

Booker does a great job advising visitors on the best time to observe the seals but cannot guarantee that they will always be there.

If you don't get to see them here, other seal populations are increasing along the Northern Irish coast, in particular in Strangford in County Down and in the Copeland Islands off the coast. Both are now home to healthy numbers of grey seals.

The Lagan Boat Company also offers tours round the Titanic Harbour and the shipyards of Harland and Wolff, as well as trips down the Holywood coast. You can also head upriver to Lanyon Quay, near the Waterfront Hall, where you can see a collection of photos, ship plans, documents and drawings pertaining to Belfast's maritime history on board the *Belfast Barge*. This is part of the Lagan Legacy charity established by Derek Booker and Joyce Anderson. Admission is free, but donations are welcome.

BIG FISH CERAMIC TILES

Ceramic tiles tell of Belfast's history

Donegall Quay, BT1 3NG
(Near the Lagan Lookout and Custom House)
Buses: 1a, 1b, 1c, 1d, 1e, 1f, 1g

Along the banks of the revamped docklands along the River Lagan, the enormous 10-metre-long ceramic sculpture of a salmon is the creation of Belfast-born artist John Kindness. He won a competition in 1999 to create this piece of public art, choosing the salmon as a symbol both of the Laganside regeneration and the peace talks underway at the time.

The more you look, the more you see on *Big Fish*. The scales are made from intricate mosaic tiles, each revealing a different aspect of Belfast's complex history.

The artist asked local schoolchildren to contribute ideas anonymously for the tiles, making it a true community project. "A huge amount of the images I selected were done by James Ratcliffe, who I found out later is severely autistic," says Kindness. "I loved his strong visual perception and accurate drawings."

Ratcliffe's drawings of Belfast's Opera House and the Albert Clock feature among the scales, as well as a particularly clever and striking image of

U2's Bono and politicians David Trimble and John Hume. The latter is in the form of a collage with the heads of the main peace process negotiators attached to basic stick figures. It is located in the section that runs into the tail. It is definitely worth getting on your hands and knees to inspect the underbelly of the fish: you'll notice enlarged images of parasites dotted about here and there, a light-hearted touch illustrating the fact that wild salmon pick up parasites that attach themselves to the scales. These are replicated from microscopic images of the actual parasite.

The tiles on the back of the fish are darker, in more ways than one, and you need to stand on tiptoes to see properly. Kindness lived through The Troubles himself, narrowly escaping a bomb blast at the Abercorn Restaurant in 1972. "You can't shy away from Belfast's violent history", he explains, "and a few of those episodes are reflected in my darker tiles."

A sunny day will highlight the gradation of colour on the tiles and their iridescence as you unravel Belfast's secrets and stories.

The white tiles reflect the city's damask linen tradition and it was during the creation of this salmon that Kindness developed a way of printing on enamel that enabled him to reflect the translucency of the fish.

Before sealing the immense steel armature of the structure, the artist invited friends to contribute items for a time capsule. Newspaper cuttings, poems and other random objects are sealed within the fish. But that's something for future generations to discover.

OH YEAH MUSIC CENTRE

A place that celebrates Belfast's contribution to popular music

15–21 Gordon Street, BT1 2LG
028 90 310845
www.ohyeahbelfast.com
Music exhibition: Mon–Fri 9am–5pm, Sat 12pm–6pm
These hours may change during quieter or busier times
Free

Behind the brick walls and industrial doorway of a former whiskey warehouse in the city's Cathedral Quarter, the modern Oh Yeah Centre is a dedicated music hub that celebrates the significant contribution that artists from Belfast have made to modern music.

Inside, an exhibition celebrates home-grown legends of rock, blues and folk such as Van Morrison, guitarist Gary Moore and The Undertones. It includes original concert memorabilia, personal items from tours, and some of these musicians' best-loved guitars. Of particular note is a vintage sign of Cyprus Avenue, birthplace of "Van the Man" Morrison, and Gary Moore's favourite guitar, donated by his family.

There is something for rap fans too: a leather jacket owned by Ad-Rock from the Beastie Boys, worn circa 1985.

It is no surprise that this hub of musical inspiration was established here: the Cathedral Quarter is a place where creative types have been coming together for centuries to perform. In 1792 an Ireland-wide harp festival took place in the nearby Assembly Rooms on Donegall Street. For aspiring musicians, this is the place to be: you may even bump into established stars from time to time.

One of the founder members of the centre is Snow Patrol's Gary Lightbody, who donated several special items to the exhibition. His Fender Telecaster Deluxe guitar, on which he wrote hits such as *Run* and *Chasing Cars*, is on display. Lightbody, like others, supported the creation of "Oh Yeah" in the belief that music is an agent for change and can genuinely enrich people's lives. The centre welcomes all ages, as proven by its Arts & Older People Programme and the summer "acoustic picnics" for families.

NEARBY

Two small cast-iron cobble plaques on the pavement outside mark the spot where King William of Orange is said to have entered the city in 1690. Curiously, the text is written in its mirror image and no one is quite sure why. Just a simple mistake?

Try out the Oh Yeah Centre's monthly Music Bus Tour to brush up on your knowledge of the Belfast music scene. It starts just outside the Ulster Hall, where Led Zeppelin introduced the world to *Stairway to Heaven* in 1971.

STATUE OF JAMES LARKIN

Rebel with a cause

Donegall Street Place, BT1 2FN

Hidden down a small alleyway in the Cathedral Quarter stands a life-size bronze figure of James Larkin (1876–1947), a renowned left-wing firebrand. The sculpture hangs on the gable wall of the Irish Congress of Trade Unions and depicts an animated Larkin, arms outstretched as if gushing forth words of encouragement to his followers.

An Irish Trade Union leader and social activist, Jim Larkin was born to Irish parents but grew up in the slums of Liverpool. On arriving in Belfast in 1907, he immediately began organising the city's dock workers into the Belfast Dock Strike and even succeeded in uniting Catholics and Protestants in a common cause. He went on to found the Irish Transport and General Workers' Union.

Larkin was an inspiring speaker and worked tirelessly to improve the condition of workers. He wanted to restore their self-respect and actively supported policies promoting social equality and justice, thereby encouraging them to aspire to greater things.

Belfast sculptor Anto Brennan, who was commissioned to make the statue, decided that Larkin was a man who was respected and esteemed on *both* sides of the political divide, making him the ideal subject. "It's a sculpture everyone can buy into," he says. "Everyone's Da or Granda was a member of the trade unions. It's a piece of art about the people and for the people." The sculpture was unveiled in 2006.

Seven years later, a huge and colourful mural by well-known Belfast muralists Danny Devanny and Mark Ervine was added to the wall directly behind the bronze figure to complement it.

It shows trade unionists carrying banners, logos and other symbols that recount the story of organised labour from the Dockers' and Carters' Strike of 1907, and the struggle of women working in the city's mills and factories, to current campaigns against austerity and for social justice.

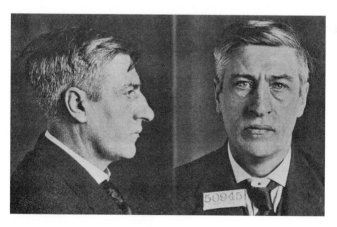

NEARBY

The John Hewitt Bar, just round the corner at 51 Donegall Street, continues the theme of social justice. John Hewitt (1907–87) was a poet, a socialist and a Freeman of Belfast. He opened the Belfast Unemployed Resource Centre in 1983. However, he was not universally popular due to his radical socialist views. Eventually, the managers at the centre decided to boost their funds by going into business, and the John Hewitt Bar opened its doors in 1999. It remains a popular meeting place for musicians, artists, writers, journalists and students.

TITANIC PALL

(19)

Stunning memorial to the Titanic *dead*

St Anne's Cathedral, Donegall Street, Belfast BT1 2HB
028 90 328332
www.belfastcathedral.org
Mon–Sat 9am–5.15pm (last audio tour 4.45pm), Sun 1pm–3pm. Closed to
visitors during services
Buses: 1a, 1c, 1d, 1e, 1f, 1g

Inside St Anne's Cathedral, along the right-hand wall, a huge and striking cloth presents a striking luminescent cross. Made from Merino wool, the beautiful pall (a cloth that is traditionally placed over a coffin) measures 3.6 × 2.4 metres. Created by textile artists Helen O'Hare and Wilma Kirkpatrick, it was designed in 2012 to commemorate the centenary of the tragic sinking of the *Titanic* in 1912.

Its true beauty is revealed in the detail: backed with Irish linen, it has 50 colours including the main midnight blue, which evokes the night sea in which the *Titanic* came to rest.

The large central cross is fashioned from hundreds of tiny crosses individually stitched in silk, rayon, metallic and cotton threads. They fall away towards the velvet edges of the pall, symbolising the lives fading away into the darkness of the icy waves.

The pall is also adorned with 1,517 hand-embroidered tiny gold crosses and a handful of Stars of David and Crescents representing each life lost. The Dean of Belfast, the Very Reverend John Mann, says, "This is a very special piece of stunning needlework that people will travel to see. Looking at the pall either from across the cathedral or seeing the detail close up, it really catches the eye. It is worth a visit to St Anne's to view this alone."

Originally meant to be a temporary exhibit, the pall still hangs in the cathedral.

The baptistery's mosaic ceiling has a beautiful image of the Creation in Romanesque style. Each of its 150,000 pieces of Italian glass was hand-painted by two London sisters, Gertrude and Margaret Martin in the 1920s and 30s. The carved stone busts of children that surround the font are the work of sculptress Rosamund Praeger (see p. 138).

The lightweight, titanium-clad Spire of Hope can be seen from both inside and outside the cathedral. It punctures the roof to poke down towards the centre of the nave, rising 40 metres above the floor and flooding the inside with natural light.

CABINET OF ST MARY'S CHURCH

A private cabinet that was used for secret Masses

Chapel Lane, BT1 1HH
028 90 320482
www.stmarysbelfast.org
Mon–Sat 7am–6pm, Sun 9am–1pm
Buses: 1, 1a, 1c, 1d

Although it looks like any regular cabinet, the one in St Mary's Church has a unique history. It comes from a private house owned by a Mr Kennedy in Castle Street: when the penal laws from the 1690s were active, it served as a makeshift altar where the parish priest would come to celebrate Mass in secret. If the house was raided by the British, the chalice and other religious items could swiftly be concealed inside the cabinet's drawers. Opened in 1784, St Mary's was the first Catholic church to be re-established in the city, at a time when the British penal laws were still in place and there was a high degree of empathy between the Irish Presbyterians and Catholics.

These penal laws prevented Catholics from participating in worship, limited their participation in politics and education and restricted their ability to own land. Catholic emancipation did not occur until 1829: at the time of the opening of the church, Belfast's Catholic population numbered fewer than four hundred. Secret Masses such as those in Kennedy's house took place in various other sites around the city. Those who attended put themselves in grave danger (see p. 100).

The cabinet has survived and is now incorporated into the altar at St Mary's. The pulpit is also of great historical interest: it's believed to originate from the old Anglican church of St George's in the High Street, and is said to have been in the church when King William of Orange passed by on his way to the Battle of the Boyne in 1690. It was presented by the Reverend Bristow, vicar of Belfast at the time, to Father O'Donnell, the priest who said the first Mass when the church opened in 1784.

A Catholic church built with Protestant money

It may be surprising to hear that in the early 18th century there was a high degree of religious tolerance in the north of Ireland. Tucked away behind the modern Castlecourt shopping centre, St Mary's Church is testament to the ecumenical nature of the city at that time: 80 per cent of the funds to build this Catholic church were donated by Protestants.

At the rear of the church, the small, peaceful garden with a Lourdes-style grotto was created in 1954 by the architect Padraic Gregory (1886–1962). It contains a stained-glass window that commemorates the church's role in protecting evacuees from the Hungarian Revolution of 1956, when protesters were killed for demonstrating against Soviet domination. In the 1940s, Gregory also created the beautiful semicircular apse within the church itself, complete with an elaborate Celtic mosaic.

EMMA STEBBINS SCULPTURES

Little-known 19th-century marble masterpieces

Central Library, Royal Avenue, BT1 1EA
028 90 509150
www.librariesni.org.uk
Mon and Thurs 9am–8pm, Tues, Wed and Fri 9am–5.30pm,
Sat 10am–4.30pm, Sun closed
Free
Buses: 1a, 1c, 1d, 1e, 1f, 1g, 1j

After ascending the iconic staircase of the Central Library, on the second-floor landing at the entrance to the music archives, you will find two underrated, small-scale masterpieces entitled *Commerce and Agriculture*.

Carved by Emma Stebbins in her Rome studio in 1864, they are at

first glance characteristically classical: you can see that Stebbins was influenced by her time working in Italy. However, like the artist herself, these sculptures were ahead of their time: their faces are modern and the sculptress resisted the urge to produce the larger-scale pieces that were fashionable at the time.

Commerce was commissioned by a prominent New York businessman who had made his fortune in the coal-mining industry.

In her book on Stebbins, the academic Elizabeth Milroy notes that a contemporary critic described the piece as the embodiment of the "whole spirit of American labour: honest, fearless, young, high-spirited, manly, dignified, respectful, and self-respecting".

Stebbins was a feminist, lesbian bohemian who relished the opportunity for creative endeavour provided by life in Italy.

In her work, she was a perfectionist who could not bear delegation; unlike many of her contemporaries, she refused studio assistants.

She was greatly encouraged by fellow artist Charlotte Cushman, who became her life partner.

From the time that Cushman became ill with terminal cancer, Stebbins never produced another sculpture.

Stebbins' own health had also been compromised from the physical demands of working with marble in dusty studios, and she died of lung disease at the age of 67.

Emma Stebbins in New York

Standing in New York's Central Park, Emma Stebbins' more celebrated public work, *Angel of the Waters*, is also known as the *Bethesda Fountain*. Created to celebrate the clean, healthy water from New York's Croton Aqueduct, it was completed in 1842. It is widely considered to be one of the greatest works of nineteenth-century American sculpture. Stebbins is buried in the Green-Wood Cemetery in Brooklyn, New York. Her grave features on a gay-themed tour. Her marble headstone has become so worn with age that her name is no longer legible. However, one might argue that this is a fitting memorial to a woman who shunned the limelight.

SIR JOHN LAVERY'S
MADONNA OF THE LAKES

A hidden art treasure by a celebrated Belfast artist

St Patrick's Church, 199 Donegall Street, BT1 2FL
028 90 324597
www.saintpatricksbelfast.org.uk
9am–7.45pm every day
Free
Buses: 1a, 1c, 1d, 1e, 1f

Amid the rather gloomy cityscape of Donegall Street, in the heart of Belfast, is a little-known art treasure by one of the city's most celebrated portrait artists, Sir John Lavery. Called *The Madonna of the Lakes*, the piece is presented as a tripartite design based on a *tableau vivant* (a group of people arranged to represent a particular scene). The Madonna stands in the centre, between St Patrick and St Brigid. The backdrop consists of imagined lakes and forests and both saints are shown tending animals. Lavery's wife, lifelong muse and celebrity socialite, Hazel Trudeau, served as the model for the majestic Madonna. The faces of the saints are those of his daughter and stepdaughter. Born in Belfast in 1856 and raised in nearby North Queen Street, Lavery returned to Belfast in 1919 and personally requested his Madonna of the Lakes be placed in a particular spot within the church where he had been baptised. This work is particularly significant as it is the only religious painting ever completed by Lavery, better known for his naval, military and royal portraiture.

The story of Lavery's request to have the piece placed here is documented in parish papers, which state that "the administrator of the church was asked to go to the reception area and meet a small, stout man who gave his name as John Lavery. He requested his wish that the picture be presented to the church of his baptism. Before going to the reception area, he had already identified a suitable spot for the painting." This spot was not available, however, because the donors of the altar in that apse would not allow it to be removed from the church. The picture was placed in the apse on the left side of the church after a major fire in 1995.

At the Ulster Museum in South Belfast, visitors can view a 34-piece collection of Lavery's work, bequeathed by him in 1929.

St Patrick's is on its way to becoming the best "art Church" in Belfast; in 2019 it will install work by Joseph Malachy Kavanagh, Lavery's contemporary, considered by some to be one of the great Irish Impressionists.

NEARBY

Upon exiting the main door of the church, turn right and walk a few steps to the rectory, you'll see a brass door with sword dents in it. Rumour has it that these were made during the Protestant marching season, by those who wanted to physically mark their opposition to the Catholic church. A political agreement reached in 1998 helped end this practice, and thereafter, paraders marched in silence for a block, on either side of the church.

CLIFTON HOUSE

A place of care and sanctuary for centuries

North Street, BT15 1EQ
Tel: 028 90 997022 – www.cliftonbelfast.com
Email lucy@cliftonbelfast.org.uk to organise a tour. Tours are held every Friday
at 3pm. Group tours and rates are available
Buses: 1e, 1f, 2d, 2e

Dating from 1771, Clifton House is one of Belfast's oldest buildings. Its Georgian architecture, pointed clock tower and ornamental iron gates set it apart from its Edwardian and Victorian neighbours. However, today it could be overlooked amidst the towering cranes of shipbuilders Harland and Woolf, and the façades of museums, cafes and shops. Originally built by the Belfast Charitable Society (the name is incorporated into the gates) as a poorhouse and infirmary, its aim was to educate children in order to lift them out of poverty. Inside its foundation stone are a copper tablet and 5 guineas, a sum its inhabitants could only dream of. The building and its grounds were often quarantined to control cholera and in the 1880s the first smallpox vaccinations in Ireland were trialled on children. Two wings were added to the original structure, one for (to quote Victorian sensibilities) "nuisance vagrants"

and the other for lunatics. In the 1920s, Clifton House became a nursing home for the "respectable poor", and previously unseen portraits of its residents were discovered in the attic. Walking around the exterior, the windows of the cellar – used as an air raid shelter during the Belfast Blitz – are still visible. The lawns and paths, and where a car park now sits, were home to a military presence, 200 years apart: first, during the Irish Rebellion in the 18th century, and then at the beginning of The Troubles in the 1960s. Today Clifton House echoes its philanthropic beginnings and operates as a residential home and social housing for elderly people.

Clifton Cemetery, now known as the New Cemetery, is located at Henry Place, which was once part of Clifton House. It resembles a garden, which was a rarity in the 18th century. The lower side of the graveyard was known as the "Cholera Plot", where thousands of victims are buried. It is marked by a rock with a plaque saying "They all had Names". Both rich and poor were laid side by side in this graveyard. A mausoleum belonging to the Dunville family, famous for their whisky distillery, was unique in that it had ceramic portraits of its inhabitants. There's a memorial to George C. Hyndman, one of the founders of the Botanic Gardens, marked by a statue of his dog. The graves of Henry Joy and Mary Ann McCracken, siblings and founders of the United Irishmen, are marked by small stones. Amongst the shrubbery there's also a blue plaque dedicated to the United Irishmen. Look out for "coffin guards" resembling iron cages, which were placed over graves as a deterrent to body snatchers.

ONE INSTANT OUT OF TIME
SCULPTURE

A tribute to Belfast's linen industry

Corner of Snugville Street and the Crumlin Road, BT13 1ND
Buses: 1a, 1c, 1d, 1e, 1f, 1g, 1j

At the Corner of Snugville Street and the Crumlin Road, *One Instant Out of Time* is a sculpture that references North Belfast's three former working mills – Ewarts, Edenderry and Brokefield – and the "shawlies" (women who worked in them).

The artwork consists of two statues carved from Kilkenny limestone that stand a metre apart. From a particular viewpoint, the two appear as one, reflecting a sense of unity and community during a time of great hardship. On the back of the sculpture, a poem by Albert Haslett recalls the millworkers at the height of the linen industry in the 1900s: "Many a day when I was young, I'd sit on my windie sill and listen to ladies sing coming home from the mill …". The streets leading up the Crumlin Road were known as "the River Streets": along the docks and shipyards, the rivers were a vital part of the economy. "If you inspect the bollards running up towards this and the other Crumlin Road sculptures, you'll see these names [of the rivers] are added onto the stone pillars," explains Jason Mulligan, the sculptor. "The local people were very proud to have the names of the Shannon, the Liffey, the Bann and the Avoca carved into the sides of their houses.

Geographically, the rivers were a unifying force as that is how the linen and the flax were transported up and down the country." Another nearby sculpture by Mulligan (on the corner of Cliftonpark Avenue and the Crumlin Road), *Winding the Warp*, has a pattern running around the conical form. Shaped like the annotation for a stitch, it was created in consultation with locals and resembles a piece of fabric: a rhythmical flow runs around it like a flowing river.

A further piece, the *Tudor Pillar*, in Tudor Place, has about a dozen small bronze plaques fixed to the back and sides. Each one has imagery and motifs documenting local stories and cultural references, some political and others lighter in tone. There is one of an old lady's dog that died while the project was ongoing and residents insisted it should appear on the artwork for poster-ity. There is also an array of stitch patterns cast in bronze after a local knitting group called the "Knit-Twits" pressed different stitches into clay at a local community centre.

WATCH-HOUSE AT SHANKILL GRAVEYARD

Remembering the time of bodysnatchers

Shankill Road, Belfast BT13 3AE
From 7.30am to dusk daily all year
Free
Buses: 11a, 11b, 11c, 11d

A striking reminder of Ireland's social history, the watch-house on the boundary wall of Shankill graveyard is a physical remnant of a small building erected in 1834. At the time of its construction, Ulstermen Burke and Hare were famously supplying bodies for medical research over in Edinburgh by stealing corpses from gravesites. It was in response to their actions that the watch-house was built. Families came themselves or paid a watchman to oversee a fresh burial plot for up to four days. Today, the watchtower has fallen into disrepair, but if you step

into the foliage, you can still see the lettering referring to the old spelling of "Shankill" as "Shankhill", which shows its age.

Don't miss the entrance stone to the graveyard that gives a visual history of this spot, spanning 1,600 years. St Patrick was thought to have built a church here and it was a significant Christian settlement in medieval times. The graveyard you see today is a tenth of its original size and, sadly, thousands of grave markers have been lost over time. However, the graves, the oldest of which dates to 1689, depict a Belfast that clearly experienced its fair share of plagues, poverty and conflict. For over 700 years, it was Belfast's main graveyard until it lost its status as city cemetery in 1869. The last burial took place here in 1934 and the graveyard finally shut in 1958.

To the left of the tower is the grave of young Walter Sterling, who died aged 14 in 1918, after enlisting to serve in the British Army in the First World War. Such was his bravery that he received full military honours on the day of his funeral. Close by, a young John Murdoch also lies buried. He was 17 when he was killed "trying to save a fellow creature" in one of the earliest sectarian incidents ever recorded in Belfast.

NEARBY

A short distance from the Shankill graveyard is St Matthew's Church, constructed in 1872 and designed in the shape of a shamrock. It is from this church that the Shankill got its old name, "Sean Cill" (Shankill being the Gaelic for "old church").

A stone that can cure warts

Sitting at the entrance to St Matthew's Church is the Bulláun Stone on a small plinth: it was recovered from the graveyard in 1911 but dates to Druidic times. The region around the church and the graveyard was, at one time, a clearing on the bank of the Farset River which has been linked to Druids. Urban myth suggests the water that gathers in the stone can magically cure warts, hence its local name, the "Wart Stone".

CRYPT AT CLONARD MONASTERY

A place of solace on the border between Catholic and Protestant neighbourhoods

1 Clonard Gardens, BT13 2RL
Every Sun in November after Mass, or with prior arrangement on:
028 90 445950
www.clonard.com
Buses: 80, 81

L ocated directly under the altar of Clonard, access to the crypt is via steep steps on the outside. The metal gate is open to the elements so it can get cold, and even with the lights on it's quite dark down there.

About 40 priests and brothers are buried here, the first in 1914 and the last in 1980 – he was the son of the church architect, J.J. McDonnell, who bears the same name.

During the Second World War, the crypt was used as an air-raid shelter by people not only from the Roman Catholic Clonard area but also from the Protestant Shankill Road area. The crypt and cellars were turned into bomb shelters for women and children. During the bombings, people prayed and sang hymns. According to guide Eugene Kelly, "It's often said that local people could not get in as there were that many Protestants in the crypt – I can't confirm that, of course."

During the recent restoration of the church, further rooms were

discovered and there are cellars which are now used for storage. More priests and brothers might have been interred here.

Of historical interest is the tomb of Brother Michael Morgan, who was accidentally shot dead in 1920 by the British Army. He was standing at a third-floor window watching as angry Loyalist mobs attacked the Clonard area. Another interesting fact is that there is no baptismal font in Clonard, which means people cannot be baptised, married or buried here as it is not considered a parish church.

The very fine mosaics that run throughout the church were designed by the French artist, Gabriel Loire, in the early 1960s. Their general theme is that of redemption as told in the books of the Old and New Testament.

The mosaics are symbolic rather than narrative. Those on the left-hand side of the church depict the Old Testament theme of salvation.

Secret talks in Parlour Four

Most people are unaware of the existence of a room called Parlour Four in Clonard Monastery, let alone know that this is where clandestine talks took place ahead of the formal Northern Irish peace process. Tours of this room are possible on request (call the phone no. given above). For all its simplicity, it holds enormous significance. It's the place where Father Alec Reid, resident of Clonard for over 40 years, persuaded then leader John Hume of the Social Democratic and Labour Party (SDLP) to engage with Sinn Fein's president, Gerry Adams. Father Reid facilitated the series of meetings between Adams and Hume in an effort to establish a "pan-Nationalist front" to enable a move towards renouncing violence in favour of negotiation. These talks ultimately transformed the political landscape of Northern Ireland and led to the first IRA ceasefire and the signing of the peace agreement in April 1998. The strategy of secret talks in Parlour Four was deemed so risky that not even resident monks had an inkling of what was afoot.

EILEEN HICKEY IRISH REPUBLICAN HISTORY MUSEUM

27

Archive of the Republican struggle from 1798 to modern times

Conway Mill Complex, Conway Street, BT13 2DE
028 90 240504
eileenhickeymuseum.com
Tues–Sat 10am–2pm. Visiting outside these hours can be arranged by phoning directly
Free (wheelchair-friendly)
Bus 10 stops at the end of Conway Street

Tucked away behind the Conway Mill, the Eileen Hickey Irish Republican History Museum was established in 2007. It is named after the first Officer Commanding of the Irish Republican Army (IRA) in Armagh prison, a women's goal. Hickey personally collected many of the items displayed here.

Interestingly, her sister Susan is one of the volunteers managing this compact museum. It tells the story of how the armed conflict was experienced by the Republican community and how they spent their time in prison, designing musical instruments, furniture and even spears and swords. Many of these artefacts are signed by fellow prisoners from this time. What is evident is the unconditional support that these prisoners enjoyed from their community, who always considered them political

prisoners. Exhibits of particular interest include a jacket worn by IRA volunteer Mairéad Farrell while in prison and political posters relating to modern conflict and the United Irish Men's rebellion of 1798. There is a blood-stained shirt on show that belonged to IRA volunteer, Tom Williams. He was arrested along with five other men and two women after the fatal shooting of a policeman in the Clonard area of Belfast. As leader of the IRA unit, Williams took responsibility for the shooting. He was hanged in Crumlin Road prison on 2 September 1942.

You will gasp at the collection of weapons that were used during the War of Independence (1919–21), and not so long ago. They range from hand-held pistols and revolvers to grenades and Russian AK-47 machine guns. For those interested in learning more about Irish Republican history, the museum also has a library.

As you enter, to your left, is a staged replica of the type of prison cell that would have been inhabited by Hickey.

It contains her original bed and many personal photographs that depict the fierce camaraderie that existed between female prisoners at the time.

There is an original cell door, etched with prison graffiti and still holding the original cell paper noting the day that Hickey was sentenced.

NEARBY

On the way out of the Eileen Hickey Irish Republican History Museum, take a look at the nearby Conway Mill building. It was one of the first linen-spinning mills to be established on the Falls Road. The mill is now one of the city's best-preserved and most important historical buildings. A thriving, unique multifunctional space used by locals, it welcomes visitors. Back in the day, the spot currently taken up by the smoking hut served as a breastfeeding shed for the women who worked here.

28

VICTORIAN ENGINEERING AT THE ROYAL VICTORIA HOSPITAL

Home to the world's first air-conditioning unit

274 Grosvenor Rd, BT12 6BA
028 90 240503
Special tours take place on European Heritage Open Days (2nd Sat in September)
Free. Hospital open 9am–5pm daily
www.belfasttrust.hscni.net/hospitals
Bus from Queen's Street near the City Hall. A special Royal Hospital bus (route 95) leaves from Donegall Square East at the side of the City Hall (weekdays only)

It is worth waiting for an Open Day to get a close-up of the Royal Victoria Hospital's hidden treasures. These comprise the world's first purpose-built air-conditioning unit, the original marbled entrance with its domed roof, an imposing statue of Queen Victoria, and the facade where patients and their families would have stood waiting for the doors to open at visiting times.

Located in the basement of this historic 19th-century hospital, the Ventilation Pump House offers visitors the chance to view the unit's (still functioning) fan, ducts and engines. In 1903, when the system was incorporated into the design of the hospital for the first time, this technology was considered the most advanced in the British Isles.

There is plenty to see outside of Open Days too, as the hospital's Victorian Corridor houses a well-preserved collection of exhibits. On display are many marble tablets that commemorate benefactors and philanthropists who helped fund the building of the hospital. The corridor offers a glimpse of Belfast at the start of the 20th century, when the city's wealthy classes were dominated by industrialists from the linen, shipping and tobacco trades. Also on view are early architectural plans, photographs and memorabilia.

A focal point for visitors is the beautiful stained-glass window of the Good Samaritan at the end of the corridor. It was commissioned by the wealthy, renowned physician Sir William Whitla, who wished to commemorate the heroic behaviour of two Ulster doctors. The four coats of arms in the window highlight the early history of the hospital and of Queen's University.

The hospital wards branching off the corridor are named after key figures. Of particular note is number 5 (opposite the entrance hall), which is dedicated to Viscountess Pirrie. The generosity of the ship-building Pirrie family meant that the hospital could open "free of debt", a fact recorded in marble here. There are other poignant tributes to those who worked at the hospital. One such individual is Alfred Anderson, a young doctor aged 25, who died in 1847. He was a house surgeon at the time of the typhus epidemic of 1847 and his colleagues erected a memorial stone to honour "his character and [in] admiration of his talents".

GEDDES STAINED-GLASS WINDOWS

Stunning stained-glass windows by a world-class Belfast artist

Assembly Buildings Conference Centre, Fisherwick Place, BT1 6DW
028 90 417200
www.assemblybuildings.co.uk
Call ahead and check the Assembly Hall is not being used for a function on the day of your visit
Free

The Assembly Buildings in the heart of Belfast city centre are home to magnificent and little-known stained-glass art by distinguished Belfast-born artist, Wilhelmina Geddes (1887–1955).

Geddes was a prominent figure in the Arts and Crafts Movement in Ireland and Britain. Several of her windows are on show in the main

Assembly Room, to the left of the centre stage, and on the stairwell as you ascend. Inspired by the 13th-century medieval glass of Chartres Cathedral, the Cuthbert Memorial *Parables* window in the main Assembly Hall was installed in 1916. It is said to be among the most striking of modern stained-glass figure works in the world. It depicts St Matthew, St John, St Joseph of Arimathea and St Stephen, as well as the parables of the Prodigal Son, the Wise Virgins, the Talents and the Good Samaritan. Nicola Gordon Bowe, Geddes' biographer, notes that the artist's "impressive use of the human figure" comes into play here, as the main figures' features, dramatic poses and subtly painted, sinewy bodies interpret the narratives

of the parables. You do not need to be an art expert to admire the brilliant, vibrant hues and colours that Geddes was famous for in this remarkable window. It is amusing to note in the artist's biography that Geddes described her choice of colour in this piece as "a little too hot". Despite her great talent, Geddes spent her life plagued by illness and mental ill health. She died impoverished in a London bedsit.

To mark the greatness of Wilhelmina Geddes, after she died aged 68, a crater on planet Mercury was named after her.

Another work by Geddes can be viewed a short distance away at the Townsend Presbyterian Church. It is entitled *Faith, Hope and Charity*. St John's Church on the Malone Road also has examples of her work but public access to this church is only allowed outside of service times.

The Assembly Buildings are home to a 40-metre-high clock tower and a bell tower housing the city's only operational peal of 12 bells that toll every quarter hour. As you visit the ground-floor shopping mall for a spot of lunch, it feels like any other modern conference and commercial retail hub. However, this building holds enormous importance for the Presbyterian community as in 1905 it operated as the headquarters and General Assembly of the Presbyterian Church in Ireland.

Hidden meanings and messages by Rita Duffy

Europa Hotel, Great Victoria Street, BT2 7AP
028 90 271066

Artworks by Rita Duffy, the ground-breaking Northern Irish artist, are dotted around the city of Belfast. Above the welcome desk at the Europa Hotel hangs an intriguing painting of a green jacket by Duffy. It has an eerie, ghost-like quality and sits next to a plaque honouring US President Bill Clinton's visit in 1995.

A Canadian visitor to Duffy's home arrived one day wearing this jacket. He claimed to have found it in a derelict part of Belfast's shipyard area. The artist noticed that the lettering "H&W", representing the Harland and Wolff shipyard, was embroidered on it, indicating that it had once been owned by a dockyard worker. She felt it was a jacket with a lot of

"spirit in it" and wanted to bring that animated element to the painting.

In this piece the jacket cuffs are rolled up, indicating that the man still has unfinished work.

As evident in many of Duffy's works, there are hidden political references to the Northern Irish conflict: the "H" on the jacket, for instance, is also reminiscent of the "H Block", a section of a local prison that held paramilitary prisoners.

In recent years, the original owner of the jacket, Willie McCracken, got in touch with the artist. She invited him to her studios and the piece was formally named "McCracken's Jacket" following their meeting.

The Public Records Office for Northern Ireland in the Titanic Quarter holds several Duffy pieces. Her most intriguing is the bronze-cast Hand of Ulster. Contained in a glass-fronted cube set into the wall, it features a letter from 1690 that records events from the Battle of the Boyne. Inside the cube, a bullet issues from a gun held by a soldier in King James' army. It appears to connect with King William on his horse. The (Protestant) civil servant who oversaw (Catholic) Duffy's work was suspicious of its meaning and requested she amend it. Duffy covered it with wallpaper. You can see a reference to the tension between the artist and what she terms "'acceptable public narratives of Belfast" in the giant photograph of a tug-of-war nearby. More Duffy art is featured opposite the family courts in Belfast. It consists of square panels with children's portraits – every panel contains scrolls of paper gathered from local children. Each holds a wish. Duffy's work is a poignant, pictorial plea for parents to always put their children first.

MONUMENT OF THE UNKNOWN WOMAN WORKER

A sculpture steeped in controversy

Europa Bus Centre, Great Victoria Street, BT2 7AP
Buses: 1, 5, 7, 7a, 10

Easily overlooked in the general melee of Great Victoria Street, two bronze women stand outside the Europa Hotel. Created to highlight the history of the former "red-light district" of Amelia Street, the monument to the "Unknown Woman Worker" was originally commissioned from artist Louise Walsh. Finding the remit offensive, she instead submitted her own idea, which was to address the underlying issues of women's low-paid jobs and unpaid housework.

Born in Cork in 1963, Walsh is an established, politically engaged artist and a fervent feminist. She recalls the awfulness of the original artistic brief and how it trivialised prostitution. "It was cartoony," she explains, "and was to figuratively represent the social history of the area, described only in terms of prostitution."

The project was halted due to a media and political controversy concerning accusations of portraying prostitution and indecency. As a result, Belfast City Council banned the work, although a private developer finally recommissioned it in 1992.

At first glance, the symbolism of this work is unclear. On closer inspection, the more you notice, the more you want to see. The details are astounding: a coat hanger between one woman's shoulder blades, a colander protruding from a right buttock, a telephone pasted onto the bosom of one woman, a typewriter on the stomach of another.

Possibly the most fun item is the infant pacifier that dangles comically from one woman's earlobe. The facial expressions denote fatigue and resignation, yet there is a strong sense of female empathy, support and strength.

One of the women encompasses all that is domestic, juxtaposed with the other symbolising work outside the home.

The Europa Hotel is famous for being the most bombed hotel in Europe.

NEARBY

Across the road, the Crown Bar (Belfast's most famous saloon) boasts an original gunmetal plate for striking matches and an antique bell system for alerting staff. The bar has period gas lighting and a highly ornate interior and exterior, notable for its polychromatic tiles. Check out the stained-glass windows that would have shielded Victorian customers from scrutiny. They feature fairies, pineapples, fleurs-de-lis and clowns.

CAREY PAINTINGS AT THE ULSTER HALL

Fable-like images of Victorian Belfast

Ulster Hall, 34 Bedford St, BT2 7FF
028 90 334400
www.ulsterhall.co.uk
Mon–Sat 9am–5pm

Located in a corridor and restored in 1989, the Carey paintings can be viewed in specially designed cabinets in the Carey Gallery on the lower north side of the Ulster Hall. The corridor isn't an obvious place to visit unless you know about the paintings, which are interesting for their reflections on the development of Belfast in the Victorian era.

Some of the pictures feature old bridges, ship-building, and the water mills that fuelled Belfast's famed linen mills. Others are more romanticised or purely imaginary, such as the Stone Age people crossing the ford that gave Belfast its name. The more realistic depictions include a view of Joy's Paper Mill. By 1903, this view had changed due to the construction of the gas works, and the area of the dam had been eclipsed by housing developments.

The paintings are the result of a collaboration between Joseph W. Carey (1859–1937) and Richard Thomson, who were more commercially inclined than fine artists, although Carey was known for his watercolour landscapes. Both had trained at the world-famous British printing company, Marcus Ward, which had opened a number of paper

mills in Belfast and Comber in the 1820s. Many of the buildings and locations recorded by the two men no longer exist in the city today.

The paintings were originally commissioned to enliven a rather drab place, and with local industry developing so rapidly at that time, they do reflect the confidence and hope present in the city at the turn of the 20th century.

Heartbeat of the Ulster Hall

The Mulholland Grand Organ was a gift to the city of Belfast in 1862 by the linen baron and Lord Mayor, Andrew Mulholland. This masterpiece of Victorian engineering is as revered and loved today as it was when it entered into the musical life of Belfast. It was built by renowned organ-makers William Hill of London. Its working components remain Victorian in origin and include over 6,000 individual pipes varying in height from nearly 10 metres down to the size of a little finger, making it the largest organ in Ireland outside of a church or cathedral.

It is also one of the most important examples of a classical pipe organ in Europe.

During the Second World War, the Ulster Hall was used as a dance hall, with the organ providing entertainment for the US troops based in the north of Ireland. Nowadays, the Mulholland Grand is used for educational programmes as well as "come and play" sessions for anyone interested in having a go.

STATUE OF BENEDICT JOSEPH LABRÉ

33

The *"beggar saint"*

St Malachy's Church, 24 Alfred Street, BT2 8EN
www.saintmalachysparish.com
Free
Tours can be arranged by calling Jim and Jo O'Hagan on: 028 9032 1713
Buses: 1, 1a, 1b, 1c, 1d, 1e, 1f, 1g, 1j

In humble contrast to the rather grand interior of St Malachy's Church, a mysterious, forlorn-looking statue stands in a small alcove to the right of the sanctuary.

St Benedict Joseph Labré was a little-known 18th-century Frenchman, nicknamed the "beggar saint". Born in 1748 near Boulogne in France, he was the eldest of a family of 15 children. In his teens, he decided to become a monk and tried to enter a number of monasteries. Sadly, he was rejected by them all and resorted to tramping the roads of Europe, becoming a figure of great ridicule. He slept in doorways, never washed and stayed with the poor and dispossessed until he dropped dead in Rome in 1783, aged 35. He was canonised in 1881 and became known thereafter as the "beggar saint". The statue has been in St Malachy's since the 1880s, but it's not clear how it arrived here. Jim O'Hagan, long-time parishioner and author of a book about the church, believes it may have been brought back from Europe by an early and well-travelled Administrator of the parish by the name of Father John Greene. Benedict Joseph remains special to the parish and there is much devotion to him locally.

Three paintings are suspended above the sanctuary. The one in the middle is particularly curious. A Swiss-Italian refugee, Felice Piccione, came to Belfast in the 1830s. He painted the pictures as a gift to the city for welcoming him. Upon closer inspection, you can make out a rather Victorian-looking gentleman with a curly grey beard, and sporting a stovepipe hat. Perhaps a sneaky self-portrait, conjectures O'Hagan (see above). In the far bottom right of the painting, a crawling child is next to a woman in baroque dress. Again, says O'Hagan, maybe it's an image of Piccione's wife and child? In any event, these figures stand in stark contrast to the biblical nature of the whole scene, which depicts the Fifth Station of the Cross.

34

MOTHER, DAUGHTER, SISTER SCULPTURE

A celebration of the hard-working women of Sandy Row

Corner of Sandy Row and Linfield Road, by the Albert Bridge, Belfast
Easy walk from the back of the Europa Bus Centre

At the corner of Sandy Row and Linfield Road, the life-size bronze statue of a stylish woman called *Mother, Daughter, Sister* was created by artist Ross Wilson (see p. 83). Unveiled in 2015, the artwork was a key element in the regeneration of a historic but neglected area.

According to Wilson, the commission entailed looking into the role of women in the family, the community and the workplace. The artist spent time discussing ideas with local women and discovered that they used to sing the 1956 Doris Day classic *Que Sera, Sera* on their way to work in the local mills. The women apparently liked the idea, as expressed in the song, of looking ahead and not being frightened of the future.

The sculpture shows a woman who is both elegant and strong. She has her hair in a net turban to show that she is ready for factory life, yet she wears a suit and carries a large handbag. She is fashionable but not afraid to get her hands dirty.

On the reverse of the statue, you can see small family heirlooms with particular significance to generations of women in this community. These include a brooch from the 1890s and other personal yet iconic objects that Wilson says "push [the woman] forward into the future".

The sculpture is set against the backdrop of a large mural depicting a gallant William of Orange that acts as a formal entry point into Sandy Row. This mural is also by Wilson, who spent a year consulting and working in close co-operation with the community to create an image that reflected the historic heritage and identity of this regenerated area. He painted the mural off-site in a barn and then had it transported to the city and placed in its current position.

To learn more about Sandy Row, contact Paul McCann of Sandy Row Tours. See www.historicsandyrow.co.uk/walking-tour or call 07909 254849. Tours depart from the King William mural.

NEARBY

Just round the corner from the sculpture is a reference to the linen industry and the locals who worked in it: a red brick sofa seat. It was created by local artist Eleanor Wheeler, who was inspired by the flax flower and cloth with a Jacquard weave pattern. It is captive behind a metal railing and therefore currently inaccessible.

On nearby Blythe Street, the Fairy Thorn Garden is home to a special hawthorn. According to local folklore, families of fairies inhabit this tree, so don't even think of cutting it down or you risk incurring their wrath …

GAMBLE LIBRARY

Home to the largest theological library in Northern Ireland

108 Botanic Avenue, BT7 1JT
028 90 205093
www.union.ac.uk
Mon–Fri 9am–4.30pm (last entry 4.15pm)
Consultation of special collections by appointment only
Buses: 7a, 7b, 7c, 7d

With its collection of approximately 65,000 books and 20,000 pamphlets, the Gamble Library within Belfast's Union Theological College is the largest theological library in Northern Ireland. Its impressive stock comprises rare books dating back to the 16th century and special collections that include the Presbyterian Mission Archive and the Magee and Assembly's Pamphlet Collections. These provide an insight into the history of the Presbyterian Church in Ireland and include letters, diaries and other documents.

Among these are letters from the first missionaries who went to spread the Gospel in India and China. The library also holds issues of *The Missionary Herald of the General Assembly of the Presbyterian Church in Ireland*, which dates back to the 1840s. These depict the lives of early missionaries and the challenges they faced. The Reverend Henry Gamble was minister of Ballywalter County Down from 1823 to 1870. In 1872 his widow bequeathed the sum of £1,500 to found the library as a memorial to her husband. She requested it be named the Gamble Library and that it hold a marble bust of her late husband. Her donation purchased 2,500 volumes costing £1,200, new doors for the Common Hall, a platform, bookcases, chairs and tables. The library was opened in April 1873. Subsequently, Mrs Gamble contributed some rare and valuable books and, in 1874, paid for gas lighting in the room.

Although the inscription states that Reverend Gamble was a student at the college, this is untrue. He completed his studies two years before the college was built.

Interestingly, the library served as the Chamber of the House of Commons for the Northern Ireland Parliament between 1921 and 1932 and the college chapel housed the Senate prior to the opening of Stormont (Northern Ireland's current seat of government). The college's classical front is built from Scrabo stone and was designed by prominent Victorian architect Charles Lanyon (1813–1889), who also designed Queen's University. Restoration work on the exterior of the college was completed in 2017.

NEARBY

Just outside the McClay Library at Queen's University you will see a bronze sculpture by Breton artist, Marc Didou, entitled *Eco*. The piece displays the artist's interest in digital imaging and represents the reflection of a head refracted in water and the sonic echo used in magnetic resonance imaging (MRI). Unfortunately, its gaping mouth has proved too tempting for passers-by, who occasionally use it as a rubbish bin. While you're here, don't forget to step inside the McClay Library to take a peek at the C.S. Lewis room (see next page).

C.S. LEWIS READING ROOM ㊱

*A door and a carpet dedicated to the creator
of Narnia*

McClay Library, College Park Ave, BT7 1LQ
028 90 976135
www.qub.ac.uk
8am–2am weekdays
Free
Buses: 8a, 8b

The McClay Library at Queen's University is not just an essential part of student life, it houses a rather special reading room dedicated to Belfast-born writer, C.S. Lewis.

You could easily miss the entrance in the general chaos of people coming and going in the tower area on the first floor. However, if you look closely, you will see a wardrobe door like no other, a replica of the enormous, beautifully carved, heavy oak doorway from the 2005 film, *The Lion, the Witch and the Wardrobe*, complete with the handles suggesting the drawer at the bottom.

Another clue as to the existence of the room is the "Narnia" carpet outside, which depicts the character of Aslan. Inside, the circular room is engraved with quotations from several of Lewis's works.

An intellectual giant of the 20th century, Clive Staples Lewis was born in Belfast in November 1898. He wrote more than 30 books but is best known for *The Chronicles of Narnia*, his series of seven fantasy novels. The city of Belfast is peppered with references to his work: the gas lamps, for instance, in the middle of Crawfordsburn Country Park and the grounds of Campbell College (where Lewis boarded) are said to have inspired the lamp post in Narnia, one of the most important landmarks in *The Lion, the Witch and the Wardrobe*. Lewis's childhood home, Little Lea, where the Lewis family lived between 1905 and 1930 and where he wrote some of his first essays, is on the Circular Road in Belfast.

Other C.S. Lewis sights in Belfast

In front of the Holywood Arches Library (4–12 Holywood Road, BT4 1NT) stands the bronze statue of Lewis's character, Digory Kirke, the hero of *The Magician's Nephew*. Made in 1997 to mark the centenary of the writer's birth, the piece by Ross Wilson is entitled *The Searcher*. It shows the life-size figure of Digory entering Narnia through the magic wardrobe. The inspiration for the work is engraved on the reverse: a letter by C.S. Lewis in response to a girl who had written to ask why Aslan, the lion and hero, had to die. The girl kept the letter for two years before deciding to donate it to the library at Queen's University, where Wilson found it while researching his C.S. Lewis commission. C.S. Lewis Square, located at the intersection of the Connswater and Comber Greenways in East Belfast, features seven permanent sculptures of characters from *The Lion, the Witch and the Wardrobe*. A blue plaque at 47 Dundela Avenue marks where the writer was born.

KILLARNEY FERN

37

A rare and endangered one-cell fern now on the road to recovery at the Tropical Ravine

Botanic Gardens, College Park, Botanic Avenue, BT7 1LP
028 90 314762
Summer (1 April–30 September) 10am–5pm
Winter (1 October–31 March) 10am–4pm
Free
By train to Botanic Railway station. Buses: 7, 8

The Botanic Gardens hide an extremely rare one-celled fern known as the "Killarney fern".

Although it is not on display, gardeners on site can show you where to see it.

Seaweed-like in appearance, its filmy leaves are delicate and translucent: put your fingers behind the leaves to appreciate their transparency.

Being only one cell thick, the fern finds it hard to survive and requires a very specific dark, moist environment.

These samples were extracted from a ravine in the Glens of Antrim. Derek Lockwood, who was responsible for lifting the fern from the ravine, explains its rather bizarre current location, in a disused toilet complex: "It's been a real headache trying to find a place to grow this fern," he laughs, "so we got a light meter from Queen's University that measures light at the quantum level and took measurements from the

ravine where the Killarney fern was found. The only place we could replicate it was in a disused staff toilet block.

"We call it 'the Bog Garden' and it's just perfect, even on hot days, as the temperature remains a constant 10 degrees and the moisture level is controlled."

Although the Victorians were avid fern collectors, this rare fern is under threat because its environment has been decimated due to farming.

"Because of its delicate structure," explains Colin Agnew, the Botanic Gardens supervisor, "it's vulnerable and fussy about where it lives.

"It can survive really cold temperatures and prefers dark corners in caves and ravines.

"Being only one cell thick, it cannot easily control its own moisture intake, and so to find it, you have to look in dark, shady corners and caves."

Staff at the gardens hope the project to reopen the Tropical Ravine House will mean that people can again enjoy a "rainforest experience" in a heritage building.

It is also hoped that the right conditions will be recreated so that the Killarney fern can be reintroduced into the ravine, thereby saving it from possible eradication.

The original Ravine House was built by the head gardener, Charles McKimm, in 1889.

MULE'S FOOT

38

A quirky souvenir from the Boer Wars

Ulster Museum, Botanic Gardens, BT9 5AB
0845 608 0000
www.nmni.com
Tues–Sun 10am–5pm, Mon closed (except for Northern Ireland Bank Holidays)
Free
Bus 8; or 20-mins walk from Belfast city centre

A somewhat peculiar object is on display in the Permanent Modern History Collection at the Ulster Museum: known as the "mule's foot", it is probably the hoof and lower leg of an African cow.

The "foot" is most likely a souvenir from the infamous Jameson Raid, a botched attempt by Dr Leander Starr Jameson, Administrator General of the Chartered Company of Matabeleland, to trigger an uprising against President Kruger in the South African Republic over the New Year weekend of 1895–96.

Jameson (1853–1917) was also known as "Doctor Jim" because he travelled to South Africa from his native Scotland to practise medicine in the mining town of Kimberley in the Northern Cape.

His decision to emigrate followed the deterioration of his health in London due to overwork.

He soon gained a reputation as a talented medical man and counted Chief Lobengula of Matabeleland as a patient.

Lobengula was delighted when Doctor Jim successfully treated him for gout, and even though he was a white man, Jameson underwent an initiation ceremony to become a valued advisor to the king.

It was also during this time that Jameson came into contact with Cecil Rhodes, the controversial imperialist, businessman and founder of Rhodesia (now Zimbabwe).

This meeting led him to undertake his disastrous uprising against the Boer South African Republic (also known as the Transvaal). The aim was ultimately to take over the gold mines.

It failed spectacularly: Jameson and the other conspirators were handed over to the British authorities and sent back to England for trial.

Although they were found guilty of treason and initially sentenced to death, this penalty was quickly commuted to fines and token prison sentences, with Jameson serving only four months of a 15-month sentence.

He returned to South Africa in 1900 and was elected Prime Minister of the Cape Colonies four years later.

The political standing of President Kruger was considerably enhanced by the international sympathy aroused by these events, which were widely regarded as examples of the arrogance of the British Empire against the Boer Republic and other small nations. The Jameson Raid, although ineffective and ill-considered, was a leading factor in the outbreak of both the Second Boer War (1899–1902) and the Second Matabeleland War (1896–97). It is not known exactly how the museum came to have the "mule's foot", but curator Dr Vivienne Pollock believes it was brought over by Irish soldiers serving in South Africa during the Second Boer War.

DEATH MASK OF UNITED IRISHMAN JAMES HOPE

39

A ghoulish way to preserve the memory of the dead

Ulster Museum, Botanic Gardens, BT9 5AB
0845 608 0000
www.nmni.com
Tues–Sun 10am–5pm. Mon closed (except for Northern Ireland Bank Holidays)
Free
Bus 8 or a 20-mins walk from Belfast city centre

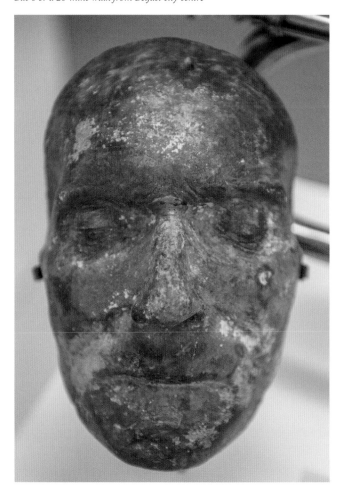

In the "Up in Arms section" of the Modern History Gallery in the Ulster Museum, you will find the death mask of James Hope, an 18th-century rebel soldier. It was donated to the museum in 1927 alongside the Volunteer tunic that he wore during the Battle of Antrim in 1798.

James "Jemmy" Hope (1764–1847) was the son of a Presbyterian linen weaver. Against the odds, he learned to read and write by going to night classes at the age of 10, and he subsequently developed a keen interest in public affairs. He was greatly influenced by the American and French Revolutions and he became convinced that the condition of the labouring class was the fundamental issue between the rulers and the people.

As a result of his social awakening, he joined the United Irishmen in 1795 and fought in the 1798 and 1803 Rebellions against British rule in Ireland. In 1798 Hope led "the Spartan Band", a detachment of weavers and labourers, into the Battle of Antrim. After the United Irish defeat, he managed to escape to Dublin and became involved in Robert Emmet's rebellion in 1803. Again, he evaded arrest and worked clandestinely in various places in the south of Ireland until 1806, when a political amnesty made it possible for him to return to Belfast. He mainly lived in obscurity and humble circumstances. He died in 1847 and is buried at Mallusk in County Antrim.

Death masks: for a person's spirit to reconnect with their body in the afterlife

Death masks are mementos of the dead: the tradition dates as far back as Ancient Egyptian times. The Egyptians believed that the death mask buried with the individual would allow the person's spirit to reconnect with their body in the afterlife. In some African tribes, it was believed that death masks could imbue the wearer with the power of the deceased. However, in Europe, during the Middle Ages, they became less of a spiritual commodity and more a way of preserving the memory of the dead. In James Hope's time, the masks were made by covering the face of the deceased in wax or plaster and allowing it to solidify. A cast was then made from this mould. However, before any wax or plaster was applied, the hair and eyebrows were covered with clay or oil so that the plaster would not stick to them.

South of the City

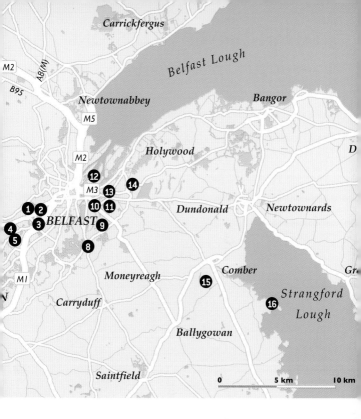

ITALIAN CARVED HEADSTONE

Italian religious traditions resonate in a West Belfast cemetery

Milltown Cemetery, 546 Falls Rd, Belfast BT12 6EQ
028 90 613972
Mon and Fri 8.30am–4pm, Tues, Wed and Thurs 9am–4pm,
Sat 8.30am–11.30am
Free
Buses: 10a, 10b, 10c, 10d, 10e

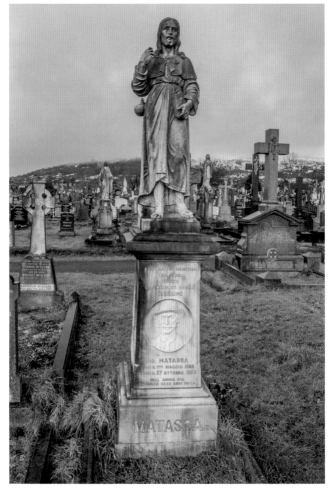

Amid the myriad sculpted headstones in the predominantly Catholic Milltown Cemetery on the Falls Road lies a beautifully carved Italian face. The gravestone of Pio Matassa, a former ice-cream vendor, depicts him sporting a neat pointed moustache, distinctive pork pie hat, smart jacket and tie. You can find his grave by asking staff at the office who will help you with location references (Matassa can be found at VA-75.B). Pio arrived in Belfast from the Lazio region, in central Italy, at the turn of the century with his wife, Carolina. By 1911, the couple had six children, four of whom were born in Belfast. Pio died when he was 54 in 1920 and his grave is marked with a statue of St James of Compostela. In the Middle Ages, it was believed that James had preached the Gospel in Spain, and after his martyrdom in Jerusalem in AD 42, his remains were taken to what is now Santiago de Compostela.

Many Italian immigrants like Matassa have been laid to rest in Milltown. They began arriving in the 1870s, fleeing the rural poverty and hardship of their villages in central Italy. Typically, a single male would arrive, establish himself, and then be followed by other family members. There were only 18 Italian-born immigrants in the city in 1871. By 1891, the number had risen to 41. They settled in Little Patrick Street, Patrick's Lane, Nelson Street and Carolina Street, bringing with them traditions that made a significant contribution to the city's economic and cultural development, and establishing an area that became known as "Little Italy". Ice-cream parlours and cafés lined the streets, and the creative energy and skill of Italian culture seeped into the Catholic churches built in the late 19th century (see p. 76). This impact on religious practice followed many Italians to their final resting place and is visible throughout Milltown in the statues of the saints they brought over with them. Examples include St Francis of Assisi (FA-55.B) and St Anthony of Padua (CB-78.B). The Italians were also the first to place photos on tombstones.

Another remarkable piece of graveyard architecture is the statue of a mother and child on a pedestal (Traversar, 0B-333.B). From afar, it looks as though it is made from stone, but on closer inspection it is actually fashioned from fibreglass. It represents Mary with the Christ child in her arms. The child has caught a bird, symbolic of the resurrection of the soul.

Historical gaps remain for many Irish-Italians. Because names were often changed in order to integrate more fully, it is sometimes hard to match them with the original names on birth certificates. It is certainly true to say that their descendants are now fully ensconced at all levels in Northern Ireland's commercial, social and civic life.

CILLINI GRAVEYARD

Where the "dangerous dead" were laid to rest

Milltown Cemetery, 546 Falls Rd, BT12 6EQ
028 90 613972
www.milltowncemetery.com
From 9am every day. Gates close for cars at 3.30pm (October–March) and
4.30pm (April–September)
Accessible on foot throughout the year
Free
Buses: 80, 81

At the back of the Milltown Cemetery, in the Bog Meadow Wetlands, the Cillini Graveyard ("Little graveyard" in Gaelic) stands in stark contrast to the ornate graves of the surrounding great and good.

Until the late 1990s, it was the practice for stillborn babies who died "in limbo" to be buried here. Catholic doctrine only allows the baptised to lie within consecrated ground, so stillborn children who could not be baptised were laid to rest in this small graveyard. Unbaptised babies were typically buried at sunrise or sundown. Mostly, fathers came carrying their infant in a shoebox and carefully placed the baby under the corrugated iron roofs concealing the mass grave. Suicides and individuals who were considered paupers were also secretly laid to rest here.

Cemetery records suggest that some 11,000 babies were buried in the bogland, although historian Toni Maguire believes there could be up to 27,000. The true numbers may never be known as the burials were not documented. Relatives fear that many more graves lie undiscovered in other parts of Milltown.

Thanks to Maguire's work, the area is now populated by tiny white crosses marking recently identified graves. The number of tributes to the dead has grown over recent years as families are traced and approximate locations of remains identified. Although not a unique phenomenon, Maguire believes the Irish way of dealing with "limbo babies" was particularly harsh. The Catholic Church discouraged parents from naming their stillborn children. However, in recent years many parents have searched for the location of lost babies whom they have named, loved, and not forgotten.

The location of these burials may also have been influenced by superstition. There was a widely held belief that the dead could harm the living, so penning them in was thought to offer some protection. Controversially, in 2000 the Catholic Church sold off 15 hectares of the land surrounding the cemetery to the Ulster Wildlife Trust for a nature reserve. This mobilised local people and historians to take action against further loss of information and the anonymisation of the area.

In the north-eastern corner of the cemetery, in Section 27, an archway inscribed with the Gaelic wording "Na Leanai" (the children) leads to a memorial garden created to honour the unmarked graves throughout Milltown.

FELONS ASSOCIATION

The only condition for membership is that you have "done time"

537 Falls Rd, BT11 9AB
028 90 619875
Daily 11am–9pm
Free
Bus: 10

From the outside, the *Cumann na Méirleach Poblachtach Éireannach* (Irish Republican Felons Association) resembles any other licensed social club. Its distinguishing feature is that membership is earned by having served time as a republican political prisoner.

Against all odds, locals and tourists alike receive the warmest of Irish welcomes. In this unique place, where every member is an expert in the history of this close-knit community, most are only too happy to sit down over a pint of Guinness to educate you further and show you the memorabilia to "fallen heroes or comrades".

The idea of establishing an association for republicans who had spent time in prison was first mooted in Belfast's Crumlin Road Jail during the 1940s, when Gerry Adams Snr and his friend Joe Campbell discussed the possibility of establishing some form of club. Some 20 years later, an inaugural meeting of the Felons took place on 21 April 1964 in the Long Bar, Cyprus Street. Up to 40 former prisoners attended.

The club prides itself on being a community and social hub for those who were affected by or involved in The Troubles. Members make sense of their past, reconnect with their families and friends, and celebrate their history and culture.

Today the club is a comfortable spot to enjoy a drink and a meal.

Notice the 32 counties of Ireland that are symbolically represented in the panels at the entrance.

The club is a step up from its former location in a dilapidated building at the rear of a nearby garage. It was a popular *shebeen* (illegal drinking spot) for local republicans.

Honorary members of the club include Nelson Mandela and Fidel Castro.

NEARBY

City Cemetery

A 5-minute walk from the Felons Club, the City Cemetery is a vast graveyard replete with an array of historical treasures. Belfast historian Tom Hartley, who has written a book on the cemetery, runs tours in August. Pop into the *Cultúrlann McAdam Ó Fiaich* cultural centre, further up the Falls Road, to find out more.

HALF MOON LAKE (*LOCH NA LEATHGHEALAÍ*)

4

Hidden retreat in the heart of a city housing estate

Suffolk Road, BT11 9RD
028 90 615319
Daily 7.15am–9.30pm
Free
Buses: 10c, 10d, 10e

Half Moon Lake is a veritable jewel in the crown of the built-up Lenadoon housing estate in the centre of West Belfast. This hidden crescent-shaped lake is in fact a former millpond which used to power machinery at the linen factory on the Suffolk Road.

History buffs and locals alike visit this secluded spot and are often seen sitting on or fishing off the numerous docks on sunny days. Other visitors can enjoy taking a break from the bustle of the city, just 10 minutes away. As you enter what the locals call "An Loch", take a few minutes to admire the mosaics by local artists and enthusiastic schoolchildren. Until recently, "the Halfie" (as Half Moon Lake is affectionately known) was a place locals associated with anti-social behaviour and

actively avoided. The community and the council have worked hard in recent years to transform and improve the area and it has now become a popular recreational oasis, replete with botanical treasures and river pike. The Lenadoon Community Centre was built around the site during the years of conflict in Northern Ireland but it remained unused and neglected for many years.

The lake nestles within just under a hectare of wooded land with footpaths, environmentally themed art pieces, benches and information panels. It even houses an edible walkway with herbs, apple, raspberry and gooseberry plants. Hard to believe, when you're enjoying the scenery here, that you could possibly be in a busy housing estate. It really feels more like the middle of the countryside.

Half Moon Lake is a source of civic pride to the local community who have invested so much in its regeneration. Sean Lennon, from the Friends of the Half Moon Lake group, sums up the aspirations of a community: "We hope that in years to come our children can eat from trees and bushes planted by their mothers and grandmothers."

> The Belfast Hills Partnership organise regular tours on Belfast's industrial heritage that include this little-known lake. Contact: 028 90 603466. www.belfasthills.org

PRIEST'S CHAIR

5

Hidden place for Catholic worship

Upper Colin Glen, Stewartstown Road, Dunmurry, Belfast
To find the "Mass rock", check out a map of the local area: http://belfasthills.
org/history-culture/history-of-the-hills/colin-glen-forest-park/

Descending a muddy slope towards a clearing in the Colin Glen Forest Park, a worship area – consisting of a priest's chair fashioned out of stone, riverbed rocks placed in a circle and an altar – slowly reveal themselves. Seventeenth-century penal laws meant that Catholic worship was banned for many years and priests were hounded and often killed by priest-hunters working for the Crown. Catholics were forced to find innovative ways to worship and thus was born the idea of creating "Mass rocks" in secluded spots throughout the countryside. Colin Glen consists of 80 hectares of mixed woodland, open grassland, waterfalls and wild flower areas. The Mass rock at the head of the glen, lying at the bottom of a hill deep in the forest, was uncovered in 2012. Local geologist and one of the people who rediscovered the rocks, Dr Des O'Reilly, says about 50 people would have descended from the surrounding hills to attend Mass here, with sentinels placed all around for protection. Their role was to warn worshippers of imminent discovery by any Redcoats (British soldiers). There were regular services here, even during daylight hours. A chalice would have been hidden somewhere on the mountain, ready to be brought out at a moment's notice.

It is a desolate spot, despite the beauty of the surrounding hills, but echoes with the comforting sound of running water.

> There are other Mass rocks in the area, more specifically on Colin Mountain and on Priest's Hill further west. Within this area, a lady by the name of Belle Steele was the trusted guardian of the chalice and the sacred vessels required for the Catholic Mass. Interestingly, she was a Protestant (Presbyterian) who sympathised with the Catholics, hiding the vessels in her house until the day she died. It is said she even hid the priest on occasion.

NEARBY

A number of fossils are on display in the Community Centre at the entrance to Colin Glen Forest Park. The oldest rocks in this glen are a mind-boggling 240 million years old; the youngest is a mere 65 million years old. More intrepid visitors can take the Hannahstown Trail, which follows the Colin River. Take the right fork downhill and cross the bridge. After approximately 10 minutes, you'll see some reddish-coloured rocks in the riverbed. These are from the Triassic Period, about 240 million years ago, a time when this entire area would have been like a searing hot desert. Further on, you see some very different rocks, this time grey in colour and often hidden by vegetation. These are still Triassic, but are a bit younger than the previous ones.

NUCLEAR BUNKER

6

Restored bunker from the Cold War

Derrylettiff Rd, Portadown, Craigavon BT62 1QU
Normally opens twice a year. Check website
www.nibunker.co.uk
Free (but visitors are asked to make a donation to the Royal Observer Corps
Association)
By car: from Junction 12 on the M1, take the turn-off signposted "Portadown/
Craigavon A4". Travel approx. 5 km until you turn right onto Derrylettiff Rd.
Approx. 300 metres up the road, you will see a bungalow and a lane leading to
a farm house on your right: the bunker is in the field half-way up this lane.

Nearly 5 metres below ground in Portadown, a mere 30-minute drive from Belfast, the fully restored nuclear bunker is a fascinating memory of the Cold War period in the 1980s. The bunker was closed in 1991 but has now been returned to its original state. Visitors descend a steep ladder and are greeted by a cosy space that features a steel bunk bed, original war memorabilia, an operations desk and various maps.

This bunker was once part of a wider network of similar structures

all over the United Kingdom – they were built to study and report the effects of nuclear explosions and any resulting radioactive fallout.

Before you travel to Portadown to see it, remember that access to the bunker is via a ladder: there is no disabled access and children younger than 15 are not allowed in below-ground areas. Anyone under the age of 18 must be accompanied by an adult. There are currently no toilet facilities and suitable clothes/footwear must be worn.

Another bunker

There is also a rectangular-shaped bunker located slap bang in the middle of one of the wealthiest parts of the city at 148 Mount Eden Park, BT9 6RB. Known as the Northern Ireland Regional War Room in the 1960s, Civil Defence Regional Control in the 1970s and the Regional Government Headquarters in the 1980s, for years Mount Eden has been largely ignored by locals. It stood empty, mysterious and inactive, in sharp contrast to the normal everyday life that surrounds it. Rumours circulated for years that it was a munitions factory, a secret school or a base for spies. Many South Belfast childhoods were spent peering through its surrounding bushes, waiting for some form of life to show. It is entirely windowless, which adds to the intrigue.

The first sign of movement occurred in 2012, when suddenly some bushes were cut back, although no one remembers seeing who did it. In 1983 anti-nuclear protestors managed to force an entry into the building, where they unearthed some intriguing details. Most notably, they found evidence that it had been used to train military professionals in civil defence in case of a nuclear war. It is currently used for storage.

KILWARLIN BATTLEFIELD GARDEN ⑦

*An ancient Greek battle depicted in the grounds
of a Moravian church*

Kilwarlin Road, Hillsborough, County Down BT26 6DZ
www.moravian.org.uk
Free
By car: approx. 2 km south-west of Hillsborough, off the A1 onto a minor road
to Corcreeny

Unique to the British Isles, the Kilwarlin Battlefield Garden was created in 1856. Amazingly, it was conceived as a reproduction of the topography of an ancient Greek battle scene. While more contemporary battlefield gardens usually memorialise conflicts fought in the not so distant past, this one, with its small but verdant grassy mounds, creates a physical model of Thermopylae (north-west of Athens), the site of a fierce battle between Persians and Greeks in 480 BC.

To truly appreciate the garden, it's useful to know the gist of what happened at Thermopylae (although each mound in the garden is marked to indicate a stage in the battle). Around the 5th century BC, the Persians and Greeks were locked in a fierce conflict. In order to force the situation,

the Persians assembled a colossal army. When the Greeks learned of its size, they decided their best chance was to delay the enemy at the bottleneck of a mountain pass at Thermopylae, so they had time to pursue the Persian navy at sea. This was effective and the two sides ended up in hand-to-hand combat. The Persians gained the upper hand when the Greeks were betrayed by Ephialtes, and a mass slaughter ensued. Many Greeks fled in terror but the heroic Spartans and some others remained. They spread out into the wider part of the pass, a move that pushed many of the Persians into the sea. Their leader was then killed and the Greeks were surrounded. They withdrew for the last time behind a wall, forming themselves into a single, compact body. One Greek scribe wrote that they "resisted to the last with their swords, and if they had them, their hands and teeth". Although these men were defeated at Thermopylae, they are remembered for their great courage in the face of impossible odds.

The garden was created by Basil Patras Zulu, a Greek refugee who participated in the 19th-century struggle for Greek independence. He later sought refuge in Ireland and became a minister of the Moravian Church, one of the oldest Protestant denominations in the world. Zulu served as a minister at Kilwarlin between 1834 and 1844.

BELVOIR FOREST PARK AND NORMAN MOTTE

The oldest oak tree in Ireland

Adjacent to Belvoir Park Golf Club, 73 Church Road, Castlereagh BT8 7AN
Buses: 77, 78, 79
By car: the park is located just off Belvoir Drive, signposted from the A55 ring road at Belvoir Road and Milltown Road
The trail is about 2.5 km, through woodland, gravel paths and some steep hills. It takes between 45 mins and 1 hr to complete

A short walk from the car park and easy to spot as it is surrounded by wooden poles, Ireland's oldest oak tree was planted in Belvoir Forest in 1642. At its largest, its girth would have measured about 9 metres.

Belvoir Forest is in fact home to a number of Ireland's oldest documented oaks. It covers 75 hectares along the south banks of the Lagan River.

You can follow a lovely trail that starts from the second path on the left and takes you past a Norman motte. The path passes the foot of the steps taking you up to the motte.

The Anglo-Norman knight John de Courcy (1150–1219) arrived in Ireland in 1176, subsequently invading Ulster and establishing settlements at Dundrum and Carrickfergus. This particular motte was part of a defensive ring of mottes helping to protect Carrickfergus. If you continue

on this path, you will come to a junction. Taking the left turn, you cross a stream. Take another left under a large pipe and follow the River Lagan. From here, you can embark across Moreland's Meadow. If you continue along this path for some distance, it meanders alongside the river, with an oak woodland on your right. Eventually it leaves the river and heads uphill through a Scots pine wooded area.

Further along, the path runs adjacent to Belvoir Golf Course. Soon you will come across a low wall around a medieval graveyard on your left. It is overgrown with ivy and difficult to access.

However, if you're brave enough to search through the undergrowth, you may be lucky and uncover some ancient stones. You may even find the tomb of one of the chieftains of the Clandeboy O'Neills (a branch of the O'Neill dynasty that settled the area in the 14th century) allegedly buried here, says archaeologist Dr Des O'Reilly.

This is also a fantastic place for bird lovers: kingfishers can be spotted along the river and it is protected by the RSPB (Royal Society for the Protection of Birds).

There are some 35 different bird species recorded in the forest: they include the blackbird, song thrush, robin, jay and wood pigeon and more unusual species such the long-eared owl.

CREGAGH GLEN
AND LISNABREENY HOUSE

A secluded glen and historic trail on the edge of East Belfast

Upper Knockbreda Road, Castlereagh BT6
www.walkni.com/walks/82/cregagh-glen/
Open dawn to dusk
Free
Buses: Metro Services 6, 30, 30a, 31 (Ormeau)
By car: entrance on Upper Knockbreda Road, just north of the Cregagh Road junction. No parking at entrance

One of the great joys of Belfast is that, within no time at all, you can escape the city and be surrounded by green fields. Despite a reference to Cregagh Glen by musician Van Morrison in his track On Hyndford Street, most locals aren't even aware of this place.

From an entrance on the Upper Knockbreda Road, it's a steep climb to the glen, but it's worth the effort for the spectacular views of the Mountains of Mourne. You don't need to rush: stop and take in the sound of nearby waterfalls or, in spring, the sight of bluebells. At the top of Cregagh Glen, cross under the Manse Road via a walkway and go into the grounds of Lisnabreeny House, childhood home of the 20th-century poet and historian Nesca Robb, renowned for her volumes on William of Orange. The wealthy and influential Robb family had a department store, Robb & Co., in Belfast. Her uncle ended up bequeathing the lot to Nesca, who donated the shop, part of Cregagh Glen and 164 acres (66 hectares) to the National Trust in 1937. The house later became a youth hostel and, with the outbreak of the Second World War, a military headquarters. There is a memorial to US servicemen who were buried here for a time, before being later exhumed. After WWII, the house fell into disrepair, only to be restored in the late 1980s by Lagan College. It reopened in 1991 as Belfast's first religiously integrated school. You can still see the ivy that climbs up the walls of what would have been Nesca's old family garden. Past Lisnabreeny House, you cross stiles, open fields and grassy tracks until you reach a circle of mature trees marking the site of an ancient fairy rath (a circular earthen wall forming an enclosure that served as a fort and residence for a tribal chief). Dating to the early Christian period (between 500 and 1000), it would have been a homestead, protecting family and livestock from wild animals and enemies. Situated as it is on the hills overlooking Belfast, with great views of routes into Strangford Lough, some people surmise that the first inhabitants may have witnessed the arrival of the Vikings.

For tourists interested in exploring more sights around East Belfast, it is worth paying a visit to the EastSide Visitor Centre at 402 Newtownards Road, BT4 1HU (www.eastsidepartnership.com). The centre has a coffee bar named after EastSide's most famous author, C.S. Lewis (see p. 83), affectionately known as "Jack" to his close friends and family.

AUNT SANDRA'S CANDY FACTORY ⑩

*One of Europe's award-winning sweet shops
with a history spanning six decades*

60 Castlereagh Rd, BT5 5FP
028 90 732868
www.auntsandras.com
Daily 10am–6pm. Shows every Sat and Sun
Buses: 1a, 1c, 1d, 1e

Children and adults alike will be irresistibly drawn to the family-run Aunt Sandra's Candy Factory, a Belfast institution that has been making old-style sweets and chocolates for the past 60 years. Its reputation relies on the word of local people, and weekend shows (strongly recommended) demonstrate how vintage sweets are still made today,

using traditional machinery. The equipment and the recipes remain largely unchanged, says current owner Jim Moore, who is known affectionately by locals as "Uncle Jim".

Queues for Aunt Sandra's goodies can be seen winding down the street, especially at certain times of the year, such as Halloween, when the small team churn out 176,000 candy apples. The double-fronted pink shop is the size of a large living room and can hold about 40 people.

In all its history, Aunt Sandra's has remained true to its origins, has never expanded and eschews the big chains to provide lucky customers with special treats. "We only ever rely on word of mouth," Uncle Jim explains, "and when people ask what we make, I always say we make people happy. That's our philosophy. We're rough and ready and don't make wee dainty things. I can't explain why, but people love it."

The story of Aunt Sandra's goes back to Uncle Willy, who, on his way to school in the 1940s would pass an old sweet factory. So divine were the smells emanating from the factory that Willy determined he would make sweets and chocolates for a living. On finishing school, he asked the factory boss for a job. Willy worked his way up the ranks but unfortunately lost three fingers to a chopping machine. He received £300 in compensation, £100 for each finger, which was a tidy sum in those days and enough to open his own sweet shop.

Two more shops followed and Uncle Willy hired an assistant. A little girl called Sandra came to work with him and stayed for the next 39 years. Hence the name "Aunt Sandra's". Sandra was the current Uncle Jim's aunt and kept the shop going for decades. Jim managed to acquire the original sweet-making equipment so that current visitors can enjoy the original confectionery recipes. For Jim, the most important aspect is that people enjoy the experience, be it a visit to the shop, a party, a special occasion or a workshop. Aunt Sandra's produces between 1.5 and 2 tonnes of sugar per week. Some of its special sweets include raspberry ruffles, Belfast fudge, Irish cream fudge and the oldest sweet in Ireland, the iconic "yellow man".

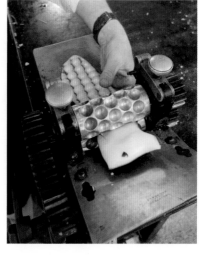

CON O'NEILL BRIDGE

The oldest surviving structure in Belfast

Abetta Parade, off the Beersbridge Road, BT5 5EH
Bus: 3A to Connswater. Get off the bus and take a right onto Bloomfield Avenue.
Walk along this route and then turn right at Beersbridge Road. Continue until
Abetta Parade

Along the Beersbridge Road, tucked in between Elmgrove Primary School and the local Pentecostal church, the Con O'Neill Bridge is reputedly the oldest surviving structure in Belfast. In ancient times, this bridge was located on the lands belonging to Con O'Neill, a 16th-century Irishman who owned much of East Ulster. The bridge lay on a track which led from the mouth of the "Conn's Water" to the O'Neill stronghold in the Castlereagh Hills. O'Neill was a great warrior and a bit of a rogue, who enjoyed raucous parties at his home. Legend has it that he and his clansmen used this bridge in the early 17th century to smuggle stolen wine from Belfast town to their castle. The exact age of the bridge is disputed, but local historian Dr Desie O'Reilly thinks it may be even older and date back to medieval times. In the mid and late 1800s, the Connswater River was the driving force behind East Belfast's industrial growth. Barges carrying goods travelled its length and its water powered many of the great mills in the local area. A major investment in East Belfast has helped this once derelict area develop into an attractive spot recognised

for its beauty and history. It is hoped that the £40 million regeneration of the area known as the Connswater Community Greenway will help attract more visitors to the area.

Van Morrison and the Con O'Neill Bridge

This small cobblestone bridge is in what locals call "The Hollow", made famous from Van Morrison's hit song, Brown-Eyed Girl. The musician grew up in this area and spent much of his childhood exploring here.

To find out more about Van Morrison's relationship to this part of the city, you can walk the Van Morrison Trail, a round trip that takes you on a journey through the East Belfast of his youth: www.communitygreenway.co.uk/vanmorrisontrail.

NEARBY

Opened to the public in 1906, Victoria Park was landscaped by Charles McKimm, who also built the Tropical Ravine House in Belfast's Botanic Gardens (see p. 84). The central area of the park has traditionally been a popular spot for football, bowling and cricket. These days, it is a designated Area of Special Scientific Interest, largely because of its abundant wildlife. The park contains walking routes and a lake originally used for small boats.

DOOR IN THE DOCK CAFÉ

A secret doorway to the Titanic *in a café with a conscience*

2k Queen's Road, on corner nearest SS Nomadic
www.the-dock.org
Daily 11am–5pm
Buses: 1a, 1c, 1d, 1e, 1f

Aerial view

In spite of its ordinary appearance, the Dock Café contains a piece of Belfast naval history that even the most ardent *Titanic* enthusiast wouldn't know about. To the rear, in a corner, is an oak door connected to Thomas Andrews, chief naval architect responsible for overseeing the design and construction of the ship (see p. 121).

The door features two small bronze plaques. One states "Doorway to the Titanic" and the other reveals that this is Andrews' actual childhood bedroom door. Andrews' early love of water and proficiency at sailing earned him the nickname "the Admiral". He was able to nurture his interest in ship-building through an early apprenticeship at the head-quarters of shipbuilders Harland and Wolff, which was owned by his uncle, Lord Pirrie. Harland and Wolff constructed many ships for the White Star Line and Andrews was involved in designing many of them. They were among the largest ships of their day, built to withstand rough transatlantic crossings. *Titanic* was the grandest of all. When the ship sailed in 1912, after three years of work, the 38-year-old Andrews was on board. The story of his heroic and frantic attempts to save the lives of others on the night the ship sank is well known in Northern Ireland: as the ship went down, he selflessly helped others to reach lifeboats and threw deckchairs overboard to those struggling in the water. Of the 2,201 people on board, only 712 were rescued. Andrews was last seen staring into space in the first-class smoking room.

Although there was no body to bury, he is remembered in Comber on his family grave with the inscription: "*Lost at sea in the foundering of the RMS Titanic 15th April 1912. Pure, just, generous, affectionate and heroic, he gave his life that others might be saved.*"

In the spirit of Thomas Andrews, the Dock Café oozes altruism: it is run entirely by volunteers. Don't expect to see prices on anything: there is an honesty box marked with a sign, "pay as you deem fit". This ethos echoes the Christian values of the place, established in 2012 by the Reverend Chris Bennett. The café is perfectly located for anyone interested in maritime history, as it's right on the waterfront next to SS *Nomadic* and within walking distance of the *Titanic* museum. It's a hearty, warm and welcoming oasis with a touch of nostalgia.

"Titanic's little sister"

Just outside the café in Hamilton Dock, the SS *Nomadic* was built to transfer passengers and mail to and from RMS *Olympic* and RMS *Titanic*. The only surviving White Star Line vessel in existence, it is exactly one quarter of the size of the *Titanic* and is often referred to as "*Titanic's little sister*".

STRAND ARTS CENTRE

The cinema shaped like a ship

152–154 Holywood Road, BT4 1NY
028 90 655830
www.strandartscentre.com
Selected Saturdays throughout the year
Buses: 20, 20a, 28, 27.
By car: 15-mins drive from the town centre

Despite a "revolving door" of owners over the years, and troubles at home and abroad, the Strand Arts Centre is a magnificent Art Deco cinema that has survived in the heart of East Belfast.

Created by local people, for local people, the cinema has been showing movies to the working classes since it first opened with a Shirley Temple classic in 1935.

The "posh" folk used to go to the nearby Astoria on the Newtownards Road, but the Strand remained popular with locals, many of whom worked at the docks.

Designed by John McBride, the cinema was heavily influenced by its proximity to the nearby Harland and Wolff shipyard: there are telltale architectural features throughout the building.

Constructed in the style of a graceful ship, with curved walls, a portholed foyer and nautical lighting features, its central auditorium feels more like the interior of an ocean liner than a cinema.

The preservation and regeneration of the cinema have been a family and community effort.

Many of the employees have worked here for over 25 years and cus-

tomers still pop in to recount early memories of coming to the Strand. Recently, one patron spoke of seeing "fireflies" coming down from the ceiling as a child, only to realise later they were the discarded cigarettes of those watching in the higher stalls.

Although the cinema now has four screens to keep abreast of modern cinematic offerings, it is Screen One, with its 250 seats, which retains the most history. Occasionally, people just ring up to book a seat in Screen One, not caring what film is showing.

Of note, says owner Mimi Turtle, is the astonishing original sound engineering in this part of the cinema.

Built before surround sound existed, people are "still blown away by the acoustics".

If you want to check out the Strand's original 35-mm film projector, the in-house film enthusiast, Alan McGurg, runs monthly heritage tours and can even teach you how to "spool and splice".

The Strand boasts a blue plaque commemorating one of the lesser known, yet most prolific Irish movie directors of the 20th century, Brian Desmond Hurst. He grew up in the surrounding streets, worked in the linen mills, fought at Gallipoli and had his first big break with John Wayne. When he returned from Hollywood, he made Ireland's first sound feature film.
See: www.briandesmondhurst.org.

REMAINS OF A BEAR PIT

A lovely country park housing the remnants of a family zoo and bear pit

Redburn Country Park, Old Holywood Road, BT4 2HL
028 91 853621
Buses: 4, 20, 20a, 27

Near the car park at the main gates of Redburn Country Park, a horseshoe-shaped enclosure is all that remains of a bear pit.

Robert Lambart Dunville (1893–1931) had a special interest in zoology and collected wild animals from all over the world: he kept them in a private zoo in the grounds of Redburn House (see below). Bruno the bear was the main attraction: he was held in the small quarry that became the bear pit. Bruno got up to all sorts of mischief, including learning to sit on some of his chain so it appeared shorter than it was. If anyone teased him, he would leap out to the full length of the chain, frightening onlookers out of their wits. One night, during a function, Robert let Bruno off his long chain to show him to the guests. He then gave the bear his dinner, which included an undisclosed amount of whiskey. Bruno was then left tethered outside. As the whiskey took effect, the bear ambled up the drive in front of the house and began scratching the bodywork of the guests' cars with his huge claws. Tiring of this, he noticed that when he sank his claws into the tyres, a delightful hissing sound emanated from them (how many cars suffered

as a result is not known). Tragically, Robert died aged just 38, from an illness contracted on his way to Johannesburg. Appropriately for his love of animals, the memorial built for him by his mother Violet was a horse trough, near the gates of Redburn House, complete with a drinking fountain and a drinking basin for dogs. Known locally as "Monty's Spout", it was a source of beautiful cool, clear water. The animals from Robert's private zoo formed the nucleus of the Belfast Zoological Gardens, which opened in 1934.

Located on an escarpment above Belfast Lough, the park has 7 km of pathways to explore. Climbing to the top of the escarpment offers spectacular views of Belfast and the South Antrim Hills.

The last of the Dunville family to live at Redburn House died in 1940, when the house was being used to accommodate members of the Women's Royal Air Force. After the war, Redburn House was abandoned, vandalised and ultimately demolished. Happily, the grounds are now open to the public as Redburn Country Park.

Many different woodland park walks can be enjoyed here, whether you're a rambler or a serious trail runner. Visitors can also explore the area on horseback: recommended bridle paths are marked but if you're going for a ride, remember to get a permit first from Crawfordsburn Country Park.

ROY SPENCE'S EXCELSIOR CINEMA

The ultimate retro cinema experience

29 Ballynichol Road, Comber BT23 5NW
028 91 872480
Open: "Whenever you like"
Booking necessary for private shows (no regular shows)
Free but donations welcome
By car: 30-mins drive from Belfast

The town of Comber is home to not just one, but two fantastic private cinemas created by twin brothers and big-screen enthusiasts, Roy and Noel Spence.

Purpose-built in 1990 and managed by Roy, the Excelsior Cinema is the smaller of the two and, although it seats a whopping 28 people, Roy is always happy to put on a show for a couple.

This small, plush, retro cinema is reminiscent of the 1950s, an era that Roy says he refuses to move on from.

He has no concern for the modern age and claims that his interest in the outside world ceased circa 1960. And who can blame him when you see the Excelsior's vintage posters of 1950s starlets, pleated cloth walls, decorative ceiling roses, original red plush "tip" seats and the endless supply of popcorn?

Despite its size and secrecy (it doesn't even have a website and there's no online booking system), Roy estimates that the cinema has 5,000 visitors every year. They include groups of elderly film-lovers who pop

in during the day, charities putting on fundraisers, romantic couples as well as sci-fi societies who make an annual pilgrimage to the cinema. Even actor, writer and TV presenter Michael Palin has stopped by.

Cinema goers are not inhibited here: when a Sherlock Holmes film is shown, people arrive with curved pipes and cloaks. When Grease plays, women come as the Pink Ladies, men as John Travolta.

Tell Roy by phone which film you wish to see. There's no need to pay: he simply asks for donations, or you can leave him a bottle of red wine. Roy encourages his visitors to eat, drink and be merry. He throws in a free choc-ice for the audience at each sitting, proudly served on an original 1950s Lyons Maid tray. Nobody is expected to rush home after the film: Roy encourages everyone to stay a while for "a natter".

NEARBY

Roy's twin, Noel, runs his own private Art Deco cinema, called the Tudor Cinema: it's two minutes away, at 22A Drumkirk Road. The brothers aren't competitive: the Tudor takes big groups and the Excelsior, the small ones. Since the twins share a birthday on Christmas Day, it's the only day their cinemas are not open for business.

Thomas Andrews, the designer of the *Titanic*, was born at Comber in 1873 and, as a boy, loved sailing on the nearby Strangford Lough. In 1912, when the iceberg hit the *Titanic*, it was Andrews who inspected the damage, reported the ship doomed and heroically helped women and children into the lifeboats. His body was never recovered (see p. 115).

NENDRUM MONASTIC SITE

A mysterious and magical island commanding great views of Strangford Lough

Mahee Island, Ringneill Road, Comber, County Down BT23 6EP
028 90 823207
https://discovernorthernireland.com/
Nendrum-Monastic-Site-Comber-Newtownards-P2877/
By car: from Belfast, take the A20 towards Newtownards, then the A22 towards Comber. Go straight through Comber and follow the signs for Mahee Island

With its breathtaking views and fantastic archaeological remains, each visit to Mahee Island uncovers more about Celtic monastic life here. Accessible via narrow winding roads, causeways and bridges, the Nendrum Monastery is divided into three concentric enclosures surrounded by stone walls which separated the community.

The central enclosure was the ritual core of the monastery. The remains of the church, round-tower and graves are still visible.

The middle enclosure was used for craft activities and was the main space where the community lived and worked. The remains of the stone platforms of wattle buildings with thatched roofs are evident in the southwest of the site, along with a rectangular building dubbed the "school" due to the number of artefacts recovered from its excavation.

The remains of the monastery lay undiscovered until the 19th century,

when the scholar and bishop William Reeves uncovered it in 1844 while on Mahee Island in search of 14th-century churches. He recognised the remains of an early medieval stone round-tower. Such towers were generally found in the vicinity of monasteries and may have been bell towers or places of refuge.

Nendrum Monastic Site is thought to have been founded in the 5th century by St Mochaoi, an associate of St Patrick who gave his name to Mahee Island. Monastic life had come to an end here by the 12th century although the place was briefly used as a Benedictine priory after the Anglo-Norman invasion of Ulster. Significant excavations in the 1920s led to the discovery of the Bell of Nendrum (an early Christian handbell), now in the Ulster Museum. Fragments of a free-standing sundial were also found at this time. It would have had nine time markers dividing daylight into eight sections and was used to mark the canonical hours for prayer (see p. 150). The Nendrum Sundial is considered the most sophisticated of the 10 currently known examples of pre-12th century Irish sundials. It has been reconstructed against the wall of the church.

Excavations in the 1990s uncovered the complex remains of two horizontal tidal mills on the foreshore that allowed the monastery to harness the power of the sea to mill grain. A linear bank of stones that form the associated mill pond are still visible at low tide. The mill served the monastery for over 150 years and was replaced circa 789 by a second mill, which remains one of the most complete examples of an early medieval mill discovered in Ireland.

North of the City

COCKLE ROW FISHERMAN'S COTTAGES

Stories of shipwrecks and pirates make this a great place for families

Located off Main Street, The Harbour, Groomsport BT19 6JR
028 91 270069
www.visitardsandnorthdown.com
April and May: Sat and Sun 11am–5pm; June–August: daily, 11am–5pm. Also open for Easter and Halloween Fun Day (last Sun in October)
School and other tour groups by appointment throughout the year
Free
Train or bus to Bangor, then short bus ride to Groomsport
By car: 30-mins drive from Belfast city centre

Probably three centuries old, two lovingly restored whitewashed fishermen's cottages stand on the seafront of Groomsport: one is an information centre, while the other is thatched, with an interior reconstructed to show what life was like in the 1600s.

With its turf-lit fire, the thatched cottage is furnished with items from the period such as a tin bath and milk churn. Stepping inside gives you a flavour of how family life was for fishermen in the 17th century; you may be lucky enough to be shown around by locals dressed in the "garb of the day". In the bedroom, a small exhibition fills you in on historical facts.

Local historian Alex Irvine explains that the cottages were built at right angles to the sea to afford some protection against the howling north wind. He says, "Unlike many today, people in the past did not want a sea-view, but rather sought shelter from the elements."

The cottages were inhabited until the 1950s, after which they were under threat of demolition. Bangor Borough Council and the European Union stepped in to provide funding for their restoration.

Groomsport Harbour was a particularly busy port in the 17th century, with both legal and illegal trading. To this end, a large watch-house was constructed at the point on the harbour (today a private house with wonderful views). By the 1840s, Groomsport had around 80 fishermen and a fleet numbering nearly 20 vessels. Its sheltered position at the mouth of the Belfast Lough resulted in the establishment of a lifeboat station here in 1858 (now a community centre). By the mid-19th century, most of the village would have been employed in agriculture, weaving and fishing. Women mainly worked as linen embroiderers, a trade known locally as "sprigging". Their housing would have resembled the cottages of Cockle Row. In 1865 the extension of the railway from Holywood to Bangor led to an improvement in the quality of life and living conditions in the village. The opening of Groomsport Road Halt (a small railway station) at Ballygrainey in 1861 meant more people could access the area, and swimming became a popular pursuit for visitors. Today the small harbour is popular with recreational sailors who moor next to Cockle Island and it's home to rare birds. The couple of thousand inhabitants of Groomsport are a busy lot and organise numerous community events throughout the year.

Free weekend family entertainment

A variety of free weekend family entertainments from April to August are hosted in the cottages. Children can take part in a range of activities, including face painting, crafts, balloon modelling and much more every weekend from 2pm to 4pm, while adults can enjoy live music, heritage and craft fairs.

NORMAN STONE SLAB

A beautiful example of an ancient stone coffin lid

North Down Museum, the Castle, Bangor BT20 4BT
028 91 271200
www.northdownmuseum.com
Tues–Sat 10am–4.30pm, Sun 12pm–4.30pm
Free
Buses: 1, 1a, 1b, 2, 3, 3a, 3c
By car: take the A2 to Bangor

Originating from the nearby Old Priory and former monastery, the Anglo-Norman coffin lid, or "grave slab", at the North Down Museum dates back to the 13th century.

The slab originates from a period when Holywood was known as "Sanctus Boscus" or "Haliwode". This sandstone lid originally lay in one of the old window openings (since blocked up) in an unknown location within the Priory graveyard.

Later, it was mounted on the exterior of the south wall of the building. In 1984 it was removed from Holywood Priory and underwent conservation work: this has ensured that the beautiful stonework is still clearly visible today.

The coffin lid was then handed over to the North Down Museum for safekeeping, along with three stone heads that have sadly not weathered as well as the coffin lid. You can see the best figure on display alongside the lid.

The central carving on top of the lid is a cross; other carvings give clues about the person interred.

On the right there is a pair of shears, which denotes a female burial (during this period, men's burials were normally marked with a sword carving). Shears were associated with women in medieval times.

For wealthy women it was a reference to needlework, and for the poor it was a reference to agricultural work.

There is also some foliage carved on the slab: each leaf represents one of this woman's 11 children.

NEARBY

The ruins of Holywood Priory stand at the junction of High Road and Victoria Road: they are all that remains of a 12th-century Anglo-Norman abbey. It was dissolved in 1541 as part of Henry VIII's dissolution of the monasteries and the lands passed into the hands of the dominant O'Neill clan. The surrounding graveyard is open daily, but to visit the Priory, prior arrangement is necessary. Call 028 91 270069 or see: www.visitardsandnorthdown.com.

SUGAR-CUBE BANGOR CASTLE SCULPTURE

③

A replica of Bangor Castle sculpted entirely from sugar

North Down Museum, Town Hall, The Castle, Bangor BT20 4BT
028 91 271200
www.northdownmuseum.com
Tues–Sat 10am–4.30pm, Sun 12am–4.30pm
Free
Buses: 1, 1a, 1b, 2, 3, 3a, 3c. By car: A2 to Bangor

In the North Down Museum in Bangor Castle, a striking scale model of the castle made entirely from sugar replicates the original 1852 design by architect William Burn.

It was created by the artist Brendan Jamison, a native of County Down, who has an international reputation for his intricate models made out of sugar. His works include models of the door of No. 10 Downing Street (currently on display behind the real door), the Great Wall of China and many cityscapes from across the United States in various locations. Some sculptures go on tour for many months.

Jamison has a keen interest in architecture and engineering and his portfolio of work reflects this. This particular commission dates back to 2011 and the artist worked with two assistants over a six-month period to complete the project.

The model is just over a metre long and half a metre tall, and is made out of 37,000 sugar cubes. If you scrutinise the mini hands on the clock tower, you will see they point to eight minutes to seven (18.52 on the 24-hour clock), which references the year Bangor Castle was built. It took Jamison about ten attempts to carve the clock's hands as they were on such a small scale and because of the delicate nature of the sugar cubes.

There are no props keeping the model intact and the roof is supported by sugar walls. The structure is held together using a special type of glue developed by the artist himself to prevent the sugar crumbling. It is protected by a Perspex bell to prevent it discolouring (and to "keep the flies off", according to Leanne Briggs, the museum assistant).

While Jamison keeps the glue recipe a closely guarded secret during works in progress, he occasionally allows members of the public to watch him at work and even to lend a hand.

The North Down Museum is housed in the former stables, laundry rooms and stores of Bangor Castle. It is surrounded by a beautiful park with a restored Victorian walled garden. The museum tells the story of the local area from the Bronze Age to the present. There are both permanent and temporary exhibitions, suitable for all ages. Belfast-born writer C.S. Lewis regularly visited this part of North Down. He particularly enjoyed the view of Belfast Lough from the grounds of Bangor Castle. As part of the C.S Lewis Centenary Celebration in 1998, a bench was unveiled to mark the spot where the writer loved to sit. For more information on C.S. Lewis, see p. 82 and p. 109.

RADIO MUSEUM

A veritable treasure trove of military artefacts

Grey Point Fort, Helen's Bay
028 91 852731
www.greypointfort.magix.net.
Summer: Mon, Wed and Fri 10am–5pm. Winter: Sat and Sun 10am–4pm
Visitors are advised to call ahead
Free
By rail to Helen's Bay train station

There is the sense of walking into a bunker when you arrive at the entrance to the intimate Radio Museum by the shores of Belfast Lough. The museum is hidden within Grey Point Fort, one of the best examples of a Second World War defence battery in the UK.

The name of the museum is a total misnomer as it contains so much more than radios: it is owner Sam Baird's private collection of 20th-century military souvenirs, focusing particularly on wartime communication – an entire wall is filled with German field phones from WWII, others with Morse code machines.

Vintage radios from the 1940s and 50s, with their stylish contours designed for British living rooms, are in stark contrast to the Soviet military naval equipment on display close by.

Every nationality seems to be represented here: Russian radar sits alongside contemporary helmets donated by British soldiers returning from Afghanistan.

A child's gas mask from WWII is presented bluntly with a doll inside

it, complete with the hand pump at the side of the mask that wartime parents must have used.

As Baird proudly stresses, "This is a hands-on museum: visitors mingle with the ex-servicemen and women who are now volunteer guides." The guides encourage visitors to try on helmets and uniforms and to peer through the machine-gun on display.

You can also have a go with a complete amateur radio kit that's up and running: enthusiasts can enjoy talking to each other across the airwaves.

The only items off-limits are the gas masks as they are now known to contain poisonous chemicals.

On a lighter note, visitors can amuse themselves with the wise words and tips found in the pocket books for WWII soldiers.

These were written for British squaddies who landed in wartime France and needed advice on how to "get on with the French".

Among the words of wisdom, you can find nuggets such as: "Don't eat the French out of house and home" and "Don't drink yourself silly. If you get the chance to drink wine, learn to take it."

NEARBY

There is a wonderful walk around the stunning Crawfordsburn Country Park, easily accessible from Grey's Point.

DELOREAN IN THE ULSTER FOLK & TRANSPORT MUSEUM

Back to the future

153 Bangor Road, Holywood BT18 0EU
028 90 428428
www.nmni.com/uftm
Tues–Fri 10am–4pm, Sat and Sun 11am-4pm, closed Mon
On the main A2 Belfast–Bangor road. Good car-parking facilities

Northern Irish people generally associate the Ulster Folk & Transport Museum with its original thatched cottages, farms and costumed characters depicting life in the early 1900s.

Few know that the adjacent transport collection features an example of one of the most iconic cars of the 1980s.

Everybody knows the movie *Back to the Future*, starring Michael J. Fox, in which his character Marty McFly travels back to 1955 in a DeLorean, turned time-machine.

Once there, he meets his parents, still teenagers, but his presence throws things out-of-whack and he must ensure they fall in love or he'll never exist.

When the Belfast DeLorean factory closed down in the late 1980s, the museum acquired the car that is now parked in the Road Transport Galleries here. It is a rare, pre-production DeLorean test car D24, registration plate RIA 7123.

It covered 50,000 miles (80,000 km) of endurance testing around

DeLorean Car, Photograph @National Museums Northern Ireland. Collection Ulster Folk and Transport Museum.

Northern Ireland roads between January and April 1981. It was driven continuously by volunteer drivers from the Ulster Automobile Club, stopping only for petrol and servicing. You can't sit in it or even touch it now, but you can admire its originality and those famous, futuristic winged doors that open upward.

DeLorean cars were designed and manufactured in Belfast but most were sold in the US. There are only a dozen or so left in Northern Ireland, so they are rather sought after and rarely seen.

A few short steps away from this one, other treats lie in store for car enthusiasts: there is a 1913 Peugeot BéBé car designed by Ettore Bugatti and an Amphicar (an amphibious convertible car) dating from 1967.

Elsewhere in the museum, a beguiling *Titanic* exhibition contains 500 original artefacts and 35 loan objects from RMS *Titanic*, including the 6-metre-long original ship plans.

After you've seen the collection of cars in the Transport Museum, visit the next-door Folk Museum, which tells the story of life in early 20th-century Ulster. A bygone era is recreated in a rural landscape of farms, cottages, traditional crops and local breeds of livestock. A typical Ulster town of the early 1900s is brought to life with homes, shops, workplaces, churches and schools.

DeLorean Car, Photograph @National Museums Northern Ireland. Collection Ulster Folk and Transport Museum.

PILLARS OF HOLYWOOD

A visual journey through 1,400 years of Holywood history

Sullivan Building, 86–88 High Street, Holywood BT18 9AE
By train from the city centre to Holywood

Located just outside the Main Library on Holywood High Street, three stunning but often overlooked stone pillars provide an intricate visual journey through Holywood's 1,400-year history.

The artist, Timothy Shutter, a science graduate, was heavily influenced by the writings of local botanist Robert Praeger who, like his sister the sculptress Rosamund Praeger (see next page), had a wild imagination.

Shutter decided to create the sculptures in 2008, inspired by the rows of gateposts that survive from mansions long since demolished. He has appropriated these for miniature buildings and their inhabitants.

Made from Dunhouse Buff sandstone, the first pillar is surmounted with a miniature Victorian mansion, like those built by the industrial elite of Belfast on the slopes of Holywood.

The house has period details such as a steeply angled roof, bay windows, and windows that decrease in size on the upper floors. The angled slab of land it is built upon is perched above an elegant octagonal pillar, the capstone being decorated with coins to represent the merchant's wealth. The miniature inhabitants access the mansion by climbing steps and ramps carefully carved into the pillar like a ribbon winding round a maypole, leading to a door to the basement. You can tell it's inhabited as the stone bushes in the back garden are well trimmed.

The next pillar depicts a church, echoing Holywood's 7th-century monastery (later a priory).

The capstone is embellished with oak leaves in reference to the ancient holy wood that covered the land when this monastery was first built. The church is protected by a long ladder for scaling the pillar that can be drawn up in times of unrest. Is there someone in the chapel? The door looks as though it is opening.

The remaining pillar refers to Holywood's Norman motte (see p. 106), which is all that remains of the castle that once housed King John.

Children in particular are instantly drawn to the miniature steps and ladders, running them up and down with their fingers and imagining that the houses on the pillars are living homes. Adults can simply enjoy the detail from a historical perspective and the incongruity of stone bushes, miniature gravestones and the inconspicuous garderobe, or "medieval toilet".

To visit the "real" Holywood Priory, simply walk to the bottom of the High Street, past the villas on the left-hand side of the road and Praeger's statue of Johnny the Jig. The Priory has an impressive graveyard where the Praeger family are laid to rest (see p. 129).

ROSAMUND PRAEGER TRAIL

Celebration of a great Irish sculptress

Holywood High Street, Holywood
028 91 27 0069
www.visitardsandnorthdown.com
Buses: 1, 1a, 1b, 2, 502, 502a

Sophia Rosamund Praeger was a celebrated Northern Irish artist, poet and writer. However, it was as a sculptress that she has left her particular mark on Belfast.

On Holywood High Street, close to the Maypole, a local landmark dating back to 1620 (the oldest of its kind in Ireland today) begins a specially designed trail, named after her.

The trail offers an unfolding sense of Praeger's contribution to local cultural life. With the sea on the left, walk approximately 100 metres from the Holywood Maypole. On the right-hand side, notice the statue of local musician Johnny the Jig playing an accordion. He sits, as if on guard, just outside the children's playground. This sculpture has its origins in a local tragedy: in 1952 a young scout called Fergus Morton was killed in traffic while on his paper round. The following year, Praeger created the sculpture, both as a tribute to him and to warn future generations of children of the dangers of the road.

Praeger spent her own childhood in Holywood and had a lifelong passion for children and children's literature. In her early career as a children's author and illustrator, she produced much-loved stories filled with wit, fantasy, animals, children and dragons. Many of her lesser-known illustrations of children at play are available to view, upon request, at Holywood Library, also located on the High Street.

At the bottom of Hibernia Street, a blue plaque marks the location of the artist's former studio. She is buried in the graveyard attached to the Priory (which itself dates back to the 12th century), at the end of the High Street, along with her brother, the distinguished naturalist Robert Lloyd.

NEARBY

At the end of this walk, the sea is just a short stroll away. In the early 1800s, this was a resort area with busy beaches and warm saltwater baths. At low tide, the remains of Holywood Pier are visible. It stood from 1869 until 1883. The pier extended half a kilometre into Belfast Lough and provided a place where steamers would dock and numerous entertainments could take place.

The nearby North Down Museum in Bangor houses the original plaster cast of the statue of Johnny the Jig. The museum is also home to two other Praeger sculptures.

There is more of Praeger's work in St Anne's Cathedral in the centre of Belfast (see p. 49).

FLAME! THE GASWORKS MUSEUM ⑧ OF IRELAND

Behind the scenes at Ireland's sole surviving coal gasworks

44 Irish Quarter West, Carrickfergus, County Antrim BT38 8AT
028 9336 9575
www.flamegasworks.co.uk
Open all year round. May–Aug: daily (except Sat) 2pm–5pm; Sept: Mon–Fri 2pm–5pm (last tour 4pm). Tours last one and a half hours. Also at other times by pre-arrangement
Free
By car: 30-mins drive to Carrickfergus from Belfast city centre

Located behind an unremarkable facade, the Flame Gasworks are an original, preserved Victorian plant. Built in 1855, the plant supplied the town with gas for 100 years. Today, the buildings house the Carrickfergus Gasworks Museum of Ireland.

One of the first things visitors see is a collection of giant "D"-shaped ovens known as "retorts", which are more than 3 metres deep. According to development officer Sharon Mushtaq, this is the largest collection of surviving horizontal retorts in Europe. Voluntary tour guide Brian McKee (whose father once managed the site) explains, in great technical detail, how the gas used to arrive on site, how the retorts were used to remove dirt such as tar and sulphur, and how gas was ultimately used in people's houses. McKee tells it from the heart and thoroughly enjoys recounting anecdotes during the tour, really bringing the experience to life.

One of his stories is about a stoker's wife who broke into the gasworks one evening because her husband had preferred to go drinking with friends instead of coming straight home. She managed to find the gas distribution lever inside the governor's house and waved it up and down so all the lights in the town dimmed and flared up repeatedly. A clear signal to her guilty husband who, realising he was in deep trouble, hurried home to make amends.

The museum also houses a fantastic array of gas-related memorabilia, ranging from gas appliances to a large assortment of cookers, irons, pokers, heaters and griddles. The modern appliances on display demonstrate how the old ways have been adapted to the natural gas we use today.

The library upstairs holds a collection of documents, drawings and other material from the 19th century. One particular curiosity is a wages ledger that has been locked shut with very heavy-duty bolts for more than a century.

ANDREW JACKSON COTTAGE ⑨

From humble Irish beginnings to the White House

2 Boneybefore, Carrickfergus, County Antrim BT38 7EQ
028 93 358241
www.midandeastantrim.gov.uk
Wed–Sun 11am–3pm. Other times by appointment
Free
Located less than 1 km north of Carrickfergus town centre; off the Larne Road
– Donaldson's Avenue, 30 mins by car from Belfast city centre

Located in the quaintly named village of Boneybefore, the Andrew Jackson Cottage is a hidden gem that has sweeping views across the Belfast Lough. It is a great place to begin a coastal road trip. The cottage was built in the 1750s in the traditional thatched Ulster-Scots style by the Donaldson family (who lived there until 1979, when it was sold to Carrickfergus Borough Council). The cottage is one of about twelve built in this style when there was an influx of lowland Scots into South East Antrim.

Of Scottish/Irish stock (Andrew's father was born in Carrickfergus), the Jackson family were not wealthy. They lived in the village, near the cottage, until they emigrated in 1765. Their son, Andrew, was born in the US two years later, somewhere on the border between North and South Carolina. He became a soldier and statesman and ended up serving as the 7th

President of the United States of America between 1829 and 1837. Inside the cottage, an extensive and informative exhibition gives an interesting insight into the life and career of Andrew Jackson (1767–1845), including furniture and other period items. Decorated as a traditional cottage with a dresser, Spongeware crockery, iron pots and griddles, the dwelling has been restored to its original state. It has an open fireplace with a daub and wattle canopy and hanging crane. Look for the blue plaque about 50 metres to the west: this marks the site of the original Jackson homestead.

US Rangers Museum

Within the grounds of the cottage is the US Rangers Museum, dedicated to the men of the first battalions of the elite American Army unit, the US Rangers. Modelled on the British Commando units, the US Rangers were volunteers who assembled in Carrickfergus in June 1942 to form one of the Second World War's most courageous and decorated units – the only US military unit ever founded on foreign soil. This tiny museum displays documents, uniforms, photographs and other memorabilia and pays tribute to their bravery: only 85 of the original 500 men survived the war. A large memorial stone marks the site where Sunnylands Camp stood, about 2.5 km from the museum site.

BLACKHEAD PATH COASTAL WALK ⑩

A stunning coastal path with abundant bird and wildlife

Whitehead, Carrickfergus BT38 9PB
By train: from City Hospital station, or any other along the Belfast–Larne line
By car: take the A2 from Carrickfergus, then park at Kennedy's Point car park, which is the start of the trail

The Blackhead Path is a bracing 4-km circular trail with gorgeous views of the Belfast Lough coastline and across the Irish Sea to the Copeland Islands. On a clear day, you may even catch a glimpse of the Scottish coast.

The path runs north-west along the shore and walkers can begin their journey at any point along Whitehead's Promenade. The first stages of the trail are fairly flat, passing coves and sea caves where there is some wonderful beachcombing to be had. Then the route begins to zigzag across the headland and climbs 45 metres so you can access Blackhead Lighthouse (this last section can be quite arduous).

On the walk, you may notice a distinct geological feature: there are a number of boulders close to the shore that are known as "Wren's Eggs". These are glacial erratics, pieces of rock that were carried hundreds of kilometres by glacial ice some 20,000 years ago.

Whitehead began to thrive when, in 1877, the architect John Lanyon designed a railway station that attracted day trippers from Belfast. By 1888, a path had been laid out towards Blackhead with seating placed along the way, as well as wooden houses for picnic parties. A number of bridges were added in 1892 at the base of the cliffs to extend the path round the headland. Not far from the Wren's Eggs are the remains of Port Davey – a thriving fishing port in the mid-19th century. It continued to be used by smaller boats up to the 1970s, but was a treacherous place and local knowledge would have been essential to access it safely. This was mainly because of the glacial erratics on the shore that meant it could only be reached at high tide. Historically, the port was used for exporting cattle, limestone and the beans that were commonly grown on Islandmagee. The view of the lighthouse over the cliffs is astonishing as it is a 16-metre tower, standing 45 metres above the high-water mark.

The steps of a lighthouse made from railway sleepers

The path, or Golden Steps, leading to the lighthouse is made from railway sleepers. It probably got its name from the bright yellow gorse bushes lining the way. The lighthouse first beamed out in 1902 and has guided many great ships, including the Titanic. It is part of the all-Ireland Great Lighthouse Trail. More information can be found at: www.greatlighthouses.com.

Wildlife is abundant here, with dolphins, basking sharks and even killer whales being spotted in the bay on occasion. Birdlife includes cormorants, kestrels, falcons and gannets, and in summer you might even catch sight of the odd lizard darting about.

GOBBINS TRAIL

The hardest place to rescue someone from in Northern Ireland

Gobbins Visitor Centre, Middle Road, Islandmagee BT40 3SX
028 93 372318
www.thegobbinscliffpath.com
By guided tour only (3 hours round trip)
By car: 40-mins drive from Belfast to the Islandmagee peninsula. By train to Whitehead from any city centre station. Short car journey from here to the visitor centre

The Gobbins Cliff Path is a beautiful coastal walk through an area of outstanding natural beauty. It reopened only in 2015, more than five decades after being abandoned and falling into disrepair. The scenery in this part of Northern Ireland is truly wild and dramatic and visitors are very much at the mercy of the elements.

The pathway takes you across a series of stainless steel walkways and bridges. You will stumble into hidden smugglers' caves and narrow tunnels. On one side, the trail hugs the cliff face, bringing you into close proximity to nesting birds.

On the other side lies the open sea and crashing waves. Needless to say, appropriate footwear is de *rigueur* and a yellow hard hat is provided by the tour organisers.

Opened in 1902, the original path was the vision of chief engineer Berkeley Dean Wise, who realised that the advent of the steam train in the 19th century meant that large numbers of people, as well as industrial goods, could now be moved in a short space of time, thereby opening up previously inaccessible parts of the country to tourism.

When the railway line was extended as far as Larne in 1862, scenic paths and rustic bridges were developed in beauty spots such as Whitehead to lure visitors at the weekend.

Eventually this remote area began attracting new residents and the previously tiny, isolated town started to flourish.

Maintaining Wise's engineering masterpiece turned out to be a spectacularly expensive undertaking. By the 1950s it had largely fallen into disrepair. Insufficient funding and The Troubles meant that it was not until 2011 that funds became available and the reimagined path could open.

NEARBY

Port Muck Harbour is a beautiful little cove on a stretch of the northwest coastline owned by the National Trust. Its caves and beaches are steeped in smugglers' tales, and an ancient monastery and castle catch the imagination. Visitors have also been known to find the odd prehistoric fossil on the beach.

Cliff walks are easily accessible and the family picnic areas enjoy spectacular views across to Muck Island, which is said to resemble the shape of a pig, hence its name. The island is now a bird sanctuary, so look out for kittiwakes and guillemots.

ST CEDMA'S CHURCH

Teach Us To Number Our Days

Church Rd, Larne, County Antrim BT40 3EU
www.larnehistoricchurchtrail.co.uk/churches/inver
Call ahead to check opening times: 028 2827 4633
By car: 30-mins drive from Belfast to Larne along the A2

The second oldest of the churches open for worship in County Antrim, St Cedma's was used as a hiding place for villagers during the Irish Rebellion of 1641. It is built from Ballygally stone and dates back to the

Plantation of Ulster (when land was confiscated by the English Crown – in this case, under James I in the 17th century).

St Cedma's gothic structure is a distinct departure from the concrete sprawl surrounding it. The entrance to the churchyard is marked by a lych-gate – a structure built to provide a dry place for a coffin to rest until the clergyman's arrival. It is inscribed with the words, "Teach Us To Number Our Days".

Passing through the gate, there are a number of tombstones lined against the walls, with recurring motifs and a preponderance of typical 18th-century carvings of swags and urns. However, one is carved with moon-like faces with teeth and another (dating from 1701) with a sand timer and a skull and crossbones.

There are also a few tombstones in a rococo style, which may have been incongruous in (then) rural Ireland but were probably a nod to those wealthy individuals who had embarked on the Grand Tour of Europe. Other tombstones belonging to the wealthy are engraved with family mottos and symbols denoting bravery in battle, as well as depictions of objects such as coronets and tiaras, which underline the person's high social status. A large number of the graves are of Ulster-Scots: these can be identified by the carvings of faces encased in wings.

In the north wall of the church, a small hole is known as the "Leper's Squint": this allowed the lepers of the parish to listen to the service and pay their tithes without entering the church. Above the window of the north wall is a stone head that is said to be modelled on St Cedma. A small door leads down to the crypt.

On the south wall, a stained-glass window depicts St Patrick and St Columba (the father of St Cedma). It was created in 1923 by Wilhelmina Geddes (see p. 68), a prominent artist and member of the Arts and Crafts Movement. Just steps away from the church is a medieval herb garden: the lavender, thyme and cat mint (presumably there is a parish cat!) grow between a cluster of tombstones. Perhaps the tiny garden is a nod to Ireland's pagan and Druidic past, which makes its presence in a Christian churchyard all the more intrigu-ing. The herb garden provides a clue to the church's origins. The original site, once a friary dating back to 1306, fell into dis-use after King Henry VIII's dissolution of the monasteries in the sixteenth century.

TIME GARDEN

Sundials, a maze and masses of fun at Carnfunnock Country Park

Carnfunnock Country Park, Coast Road, Larne BT40 2QG
028 28 262471
www.carnfunnock.co.uk
Open spring/summer 9am–dusk (July–August 9am–9pm), autumn/winter 9am–4.30pm. Closed Christmas Day. Certain attractions and activities are seasonal
Walled Garden and Maze are free, otherwise see website for activities and prices
Buses: 162, 252 (seasonal)
By car: approx. 30 km from Belfast. A parking charge applies at certain times of year

The Walled Garden at Carnfunnock Country Park, a secluded oasis of calm built in the early 1850s, was a kitchen garden from the Second World War up to 1957. Within it, the magical Time Garden is designed as a living clock face, where time is measured and represented by a collection of beautiful sundials as well as the plants and flowers on display throughout the seasons.

The Optical Dial works in the summer when the sun is above the equator and shows British Summer Time, whereas the Human Sundial needs a person to stand on the stone of the current month with their back to the sun. The end of their shadow will fall on the curved line of stones showing the hours. The Nendrum Dial (see p. 123) was designed by Irish monks to indicate prayer time. It takes its name from the place near Comber in County Down where the original is sited.

Known locally as "the Cherub", the lovely Clown Dial shows a beautiful carved face playing a flute. You tell the time by observing where the shadow of the flute falls.

A maze in the shape of Northern Ireland

Another nearby treasure to puzzle over is a maze in the shape of Northern Ireland, planted in 1986 to celebrate the International Year of the Maze (1991) with 1,500 hornbeam bushes, which have an expected lifespan of 150 years. Larne marks the entrance to the maze and represents the "Gateway to Northern Ireland", with other pathways taking visitors through the different counties of Ulster. The Maze is open from spring through to October.

Originally part of the estate of the Dixon family – generous benefactors with a longstanding connection to Larne – Carnfunnock Country Park has over 191 hectares of mixed woodland, colourful gardens, spectacular coastline and panoramic views of the Antrim coast and North Channel. Besides the scenery, the park hosts numerous family activities, including a maritime themed outdoor adventure playground, a Family Fun Zone, a golf driving range, way-marked walks, geocaching and orienteering opportunities. Families can choose to picnic in a host of beautiful spots, including the Wildlife Garden or the Walled Garden. Happily, it is open all year round, subject to ground conditions.

ST PATRICK'S CHURCH STAINED-GLASS WINDOWS

One of the finest stained-glass windows in Ireland

Cairncastle, Ballymulluck Road, Larne BT40
028 28 262443 www.connor.anglican.org
By car: 30-mins drive from Belfast. From Larne, take the coast road out
towards Glenarm. At Ballygally village, turn left at the hotel

Previously the site of a medieval church dating from 1306, the current quaint St Patrick's Church was established here in 1815. Evidence of the ancient site to the north-west is still visible; its location is marked by a depression in the surface of the churchyard.

St Patrick's is known locally for its gorgeous stained glass and baptismal font. The beautiful stained-glass east window depicts St Patrick tending sheep on Slemish Mountain and was made by the famed Mayer Company in Germany. Other local figures commemorated in the stained-glass windows include Captain John Park, a former ship's master on the local ferries, and famed philanthropists Sir Thomas and Lady Dixon (see p. 151).

A font used by Jonathan Swift

The font is also of historical interest because it was used by Jonathan Swift (see p. 167) when he was Dean of a nearby church in 1695. Swift used the font, as did his counterpart, Lemuel Matthews in 1683, after whom Swift named Lemuel Gulliver, the hero of *Gulliver's Travels*.

A 16th-century tree

The churchyard adjacent to the church has been a burial ground since medieval times. However, one of its most important features is a distinguished-looking tree. According to folklore, this grand Spanish Chestnut sprouted from the grave of a sailor who washed up on the beach below Cairncastle in 1588, following the defeat of the Spanish Armada. The sailor's remains were discovered by locals, who buried him. Sailors were known to carry chestnuts in their pockets to ward off scurvy. After his death, it is believed that one germinated and grew into the giant tree that can be seen today. Samples of the tree have been analysed and found to date back to the 16th century, giving credence to this local legend.

NEARBY

Matties Meeting House (https://matties.co.uk/) is a great nearby spot to eat. Popular with the locals, you can still see the dents on the bar where they used to cut tobacco. If you have an appetite for viewing more historic churches in the area, check out: www.larnehistoricchurchtrail. co.uk. Of particular note on this trail is St Cedma's with its lychgate, a structure that provided a dry place for a coffin to rest on the way to church (see p. 148), and its "Leper's Squint", a narrow window in the north wall from which lepers would listen to the service outside (see p. 149). Glenarm Friary is also particularly fascinating, as the church there is the earliest known example of Strawberry Hill gothic architecture in an ecclesiastical building in Ireland.

KNOCKDHU PROMONTORY FORT ⑮

An enigmatic Bronze Age promontory fort
on a magnetic mountain

Ballycoose Road, Cairncastle village, County Antrim
By car: 20-mins drive from Belfast city centre
Park in Ballycoose car park

The hike to reach the ancient burial site of Knockdhu offers spectacular views on a clear day across to Scotland's Mull of Kintyre and the islands of Islay and Jura. The whole surrounding area is an archaeological treasure chest of great significance: many prehistoric monuments have been uncovered here.

To reach the area, head up the glen to your right as you face the sea and continue up past Ballygally village. As you ascend, you pass a series of circular trenches known as the Linford Burroughs. The two groups would have made up a Bronze Age burial site.

Due to its position on a headland towering over the Antrim coast, it's thought the fort was used for defensive purposes. Given the proximity of Scotland just 30 km across the sea, archaeologists believe the inhabitants were probably traders. The Bronze Age is important in Irish history as it heralded the Celtic civilisation.

The soil here is basalt, therefore magnetic. A flint-rich mine has recently unearthed lumps of flint fashioned into Stone or Bronze Age tools.

The whole Knockdhu area is equal in length to three football pitches, with a V-shape path that leads to the entrance of the settlement. Paving

stones were uncovered beneath the grass, confirming that the entrance led to an impressive Bronze Age street. There would have been a processional coastal path leading up to the entrance, but you'll have to use your imagination to recreate it as the only visible remains are the ridges in the grass and a mound in the centre.

Knockdhu's history as a 4,000-year-old Bronze Age fort was uncovered relatively recently. However, there is evidence of the existence of at least 20 roundhouses that would have been home to approximately 150 people, who survived using little more than flint tools.

NEARBY
1,500-year-old tunnels

Descending the hillside towards Ballygally, there is an underground chamber, or *souterrain*, at the foot of the hill. The entrance is a tight squeeze and the tunnels are not suitable if you're claustrophobic. You can descend about 50 metres underground: the tunnels branch off in different directions and you can stand in the final chamber. The tunnels resemble underground trenches from the First World War, but are known to be at least 1,500 years old.

It's thought they were used for storage or for shelter against invading clans. Seamus Milliken of Milliken Tours can show you the way. For tailored tours, see www.millikentoursireland.com. Tel: 028 2858 3355.

GLENARM FRIARY

One of the oldest graveyards in Ireland

The Cloney, Glenarm BT44 OBD
www.larnehistoricchurchtrail.co.uk/churches/glenarm
Call ahead for opening times: 028 28 262443
By car: 30-mins drive from Belfast on the M2 and A8

Surrounded by the sea, with views of Scotland and the Glens of
Antrim, Glenarm Friary dates back to 1465 but has been reduced
to a few stones hidden among the uneven ground of an old and unmain-

tained graveyard. The friary stands in the grounds of St Patrick's Church, which was built in 1760 in a gothic style (the vision of Lady Antrim, who dreamed of fairy-tale towers and exorcised ghosts before expelling them to the attic of Glenarm Castle). The original stone from the friary was used to build St Patrick's, although some of the stone carved with Celtic designs is also kept in the church.

The walls surrounding the church and graveyard are the original walls that enclosed the friary, constructed in the fifteenth century by Scottish stonemasons. If the gate is locked, it is easy to climb over the wall. Locating the friary ruins is not for the faint-hearted, as the ground collapses in random spots due to the mass pits used to bury those who died from cholera and plague. As one of the oldest graveyards in Ireland, there are many unmarked and mass graves, hidden at first glance but evident from undulations in the grass. Some say bodies of drowned sailors from the Spanish Armada are buried there.

Individuals from all denominations were buried in the graveyard – this was extraordinary in the days of strict religious divides. Perhaps the graveyard's most famous, or infamous, dweller is Shane O'Neill, chief of the O'Neill clan and enemy of the MacDonnells (the Earls of Antrim of Glenarm Castle). His headless body is said to have been buried here in 1567.

The place is also believed to have been a meeting place for fairies: they went to battle in Glenarm and were never seen again.

From inside the church, the stained-glass window closest to the Mac-Donnell family pew tells how the MacDonnells are not only descended from Milesius, King of Spain, but are connected to the Pharaoh's daughter who found Moses among the bulrushes of the Nile.

Embedded inside the church walls are the remains of MacCreavan, a disciple of St Patrick.

A few steps away from the friary on Toberwine Street is the old courthouse, once part of the original Glenarm Castle, and one-time home of Mariga Guinness (née Princess Marie-Gabrielle von Urach), part of the influential Guinness family and pillar of the Georgian Society.

Mariga discovered a skeleton under the floor of the outhouse that she put in a box and kept in the bathroom.

BONAMARGY FRIARY

Ballycastle's black nun and a Coptic cross on the roadside

Ballycastle, County Antrim BT54 6QP
(Off Ballycastle/Cushendall Coast Road)
By car: on A2, 1 km east of Ballycastle

Along the Cushendall Road, with sweeping views across to Rathlin Island and up towards Fairhead and the mountain of Knocklayde, lie the sandstone ruins of the 15th-century Bonamargy Friary, now set within the Ballycastle Golf Club. It is beautiful here, especially if you visit when the daffodils and snowdrops are in bloom. Accessed via several high steps, the whole site is about the size of a football pitch. The area includes a grave-yard containing war graves from both World Wars. Sailors from two ship-wrecks are also buried here: the HMS *Racoon* was lost in a snow blizzard off the Garvan Isles in 1918 while travelling from Liverpool to Lough Swilly; and the HMS *Viknor* was on active patrol duty in heavy seas off Tory Island in 1915 when she struck a German mine. There were no survivors from either tragedy. You can also find the grave of Private J. Griffin, along with a number of unnamed graves. Locals subsequently erected a Celtic cross as a memorial to those who lost their lives in the area. Built in 1485 by the MacQuillan family, the friary was taken over by the Franciscans of the Third Order in 1626. The Franciscans are credited with educating, feeding and clothing the poor, and they protected Scots who were turning

to the Catholic faith. If you were a traveller and arrived at the gatehouse late at night, you would be given a bed and cared for. The gatehouse was a small square structure, and it is these ruins that you walk through to gain access to the site. In the walls of a nave, near the west gable of the chapel, the crude cross with a hole in it (perhaps a pagan holestone: see p. 178) marks the grave of Julia MacQuillan, who lived at the monastery and was known locally as "the Black Nun". Legend has it that Julia foretold a number of events, including the coming of the "iron horse" (now believed to be the arrival of the railway). She was apparently murdered on the stone stairs of the friary. Her ghost is said to haunt the steps at night. From 1641 the friary began to fall into decline but remained in use until the 18th century.

The last friars left in 1790. In the late 19th and early 20th centuries, people from the nearby workhouse were buried here too.

NEARBY

A little further down the road, opposite the Colliers Hall B&B, stands a small, crudely fashioned stone cross. If you stop to take a closer look, you will see a bishop's crozier and a Coptic staff called a "*pau*". Very little is known about the origins of this cross except that it was dug up in an adjacent field and re-erected here. Local historian Danny Morgan thinks this would have happened around 1740, and that the cross actually dates from the time of St Patrick, who was active as a missionary in Ireland during the second half of the 5th century. The Coptic Christians are known to have predated this time, and at least one missionary died here.

THE MARCONI CONNECTION

Marconi's wireless messaging experiments carried out on the Northern Irish coast

Ballycastle and Rathlin Island
An hour's drive north of Belfast on the M2 to Ballycastle. Ferries to Rathlin Island

Guglielmo Marconi, the pioneering engineer and inventor of the radio, undertook some of his earliest experiments in Northern Ireland. In 1898 he visited the village of Ballycastle to carry out a series of wireless transmission experiments with his assistant George Kemp. The spire of the village church provided an excellent location for an aerial that could connect Rathlin Island to land across the water. Rathlin was important because all shipping from America or Canada passed by Rathlin East Lighthouse on the way to Liverpool, Glasgow or Belfast.

In the summer of 1898, Kemp and a team of locals secured a mast at the East Lighthouse between Rathlin and Ballycastle.

The reception was poor, so they used a higher mast at White Lodge or Kenmara House (now a B&B).

Today, within walking distance of Ballycastle seafront, there is a house called "Marconi's Cottage", which, contrary to popular belief, is not where the great man stayed.

In reality, he and the wireless engineers lodged at the Antrim Arms Hotel in town.

Another mark of Marconi's visit is a memorial on the seafront. And at Rathlin, you will find a concrete block at the East Lighthouse that was

used to support the aerial in the experiments. The block is marked with the inscription "Lloyds Insurance of London" as the firm underwrote Marconi's work here.

By 1900, Marconi had taken out his famous patent No. 7777 for "tuned or syntonic telegraphy", but the system was not widely adopted until 1905.

There are conflicting stories as to the actual birth of radio but there is no doubt these experimental transmissions guaranteed the historical link between Ballycastle and pioneering developments in wireless telegraphy.

Marconi was born in Bologna, Italy, in 1874 to a noble family, but his mother Annie Jameson was Irish (her family owned the Jameson Whiskey Distillery). Marconi was only 20 when he began undertaking telegraphic experiments in his attic at home: his father was so impressed that he began to fund his son's wireless communications investigations. The *Titanic* famously had the largest set of Marconi Company wireless equipment in the world. When the ship hit the iceberg and began to sink, Marconi operators sent distress signals across the Atlantic.

FORTWILLIAM ORNAMENTAL GATES

A mini Arc de Triomphe *in Belfast*

Fortwilliam, Shore Road, BT15
By car: along the M2, exiting at the Shore Road, follow the directions to
Fortwilliam Park. Turn left towards the city on the Shore Road. The Shore Road
gates are on the right-hand side at the bottom of Fortwilliam Park at the first
traffic lights

As you travel along the Shore Road in North Belfast, two sets of gates mark the entry and exit to what was historically a very exclusive area, housing many of the city's richest and most successful merchants. Designed by William Barre, the Shore Road gates are in a classical style, whereas the smaller set of ornamental gates nearby, at the end of the Antrim Road, are in the gothic style.

According to local historian Dr Des O'Reilly, the Shore Road gates are "complete" in the sense that they remain connected either side. This is not the case at the Antrim Road end, where one of the pillars has been removed to Grovelands within Musgrave Park, in the south of the city.

These gates provide a fascinating insight into the desirability of this North Belfast postcode in the late 1800s, when exclusive villas would have lined the streets.

In 1877 the street directory listed some of Belfast's most eminent businessmen as residents of Fortwilliam Park: wine, wire, ship and linen merchants had their main residences here. It was a wealthy banker,

William Valentine, who had the pillars erected in the 1860s, probably to ensure neighbourhood security and possibly to help mark a grand entrance to the magnificent Fortwilliam House (circa 1830), which used to stand at the Antrim Road end. Sadly, this building no longer exists.

William Barre also designed a nearby Presbyterian church that is now the Duncairn Centre for Culture and Arts. The church reopened as a state-of-the-art cultural venue in 2014 but, as a listed building, the original structure remains intact. This centre hosts a wide variety of events, including theatre, photography, concerts, exhibitions, classes and workshops. You can even attend a fiddle-making class. The Duncairn Centre for Culture and Arts, Duncairn Avenue, BT14 6BP. Tel: 028 90 747114. www.theduncairn.com or www.174trust.org.

William Barre's other designs include the city's landmark Albert Memorial Clock (1869), situated in Queen's Square, in the city centre.

Remains of a plane that crashed on the hill in 1944 ...

Belfast Castle, Antrim Rd, Belfast, Antrim, BT15 5GR
028 90 776925
www.belfastcastle.co.uk
Tues–Sat 12pm–9pm, Sun and Mon 12.30pm–4pm
Free
Buses: 1a and 1g from Royal Avenue

If you don't head to the loo or make a pit stop for Irish scones in the Cellar Restaurant of Belfast Castle, you might not find the "Crash on the Hill" artefacts. In June 1944, a Boeing B-17 known as "the Flying Fortress" crashed straight into Cave Hill, killing all 10 crew members on board. The plane had come from the US to assist in the Allied war effort. It had briefly stopped in Iceland and had been preparing to land at the nearby Air Force base at Nutts Corner. Tragically, fog severely affected visibility, and local people witnessed the plane crashing into the hill. Afterwards, many people came across items that had been dispersed by the explosion. Children discovered machine-gun-belt ammunition and, according to one local source, the police toured nearby schools threatening a terrible fate if the children did not hand their finds over to the authorities. Today, the collection of these items includes an extraordinary array of personal belongings from the

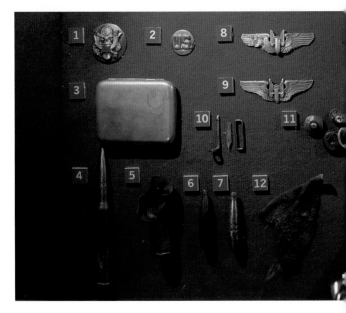

site: US identification badges and pieces of uniform, the gold clip from a Parker pen, cigarette cases, machine-gun shells and fragments of silk parachutes act as poignant reminders of the lives lost.

A wedding ring reunited 49 years later ...

A 43-year-old local man, Alfie Montgomery, found a wedding ring at the site in 1993. After some research, he discovered it had belonged to one of the Boeing's crewmen, Staff Sergeant Larry Dundon, who came from Ohio. Alfie famously made a journey to reunite the ring with Larry's widow. The story of Alfie's journey to trace her was made into a film called *Closing the Ring* in 2007. Directed by Richard Attenborough, it features the actress Shirley MacLaine.

NEARBY

As you emerge from the Cellar Restaurant up the steps, don't miss the stunning Cat Garden, from where there is a panoramic view over Belfast. Myth has it that the castle will be safe as long as cats reside there. Aside from real cats, nine hidden cats lurk among the foliage. They come in the form of sculptures, garden furniture and mosaics. The trickiest to locate is imprinted on a black bench overlooking the central water fountain.

NAPOLEON'S NOSE

The sleeping giant that inspired Gulliver's Travels?

Cave Hill, Antrim Rd, Belfast, Newtownabbey BT5 5GR
Bus: 61 from Queen's Street, Belfast

One particular feature of Belfast's Cave Hill is a bulging outcrop looking like the outline of a sleeping giant. Said to resemble the profile of the famous French emperor, it is called "Napoleon's Nose" and can be seen from most parts of the city on a clear day.

It is believed that around 1720 Jonathan Swift (see below) spotted the "sleeping giant" while travelling in his horse-drawn carriage into Belfast city from his nearby parishes in Ballynure and Kilroot and got inspiration for his famous 1726 book, Gulliver's Travels.

Around this time, it is also thought that Swift came across the name "Lilliput Farm", which was on the York Road on the outskirts of Belfast. He later adopted the name "Lilliput" for the most famous of the lands visited by Gulliver.

Swift also had a romantic connection with Belfast: he fell in love with Jayne Waring, daughter of William Waring, who leased a tannery on the street that now bears his name. Jayne, also called "Varina" by Swift, spurned his advances and turned down a proposal of marriage. This rejection hastened Swift's return to Dublin, where he subsequently became Dean of St Patrick's Cathedral.

The walk up Cave Hill is challenging at times, but well worth the

effort as the views from the top on a sunny day are spectacular. Historically, this is one of the earliest known settled spots in the area, harking back to the Stone Age, when the steep slopes would have provided much-needed defence against attack from wild animals or enemy tribes. During the Second World War, the caves provided shelter from bombing raids for the local population.

When exploring the area today, keep an eager eye out for magnificent peregrine falcons, kestrels and other birds of prey that come and hunt over the mountain tops.

A clergyman as well as a satirist, essayist and poet, Jonathan Swift (1667–1745) is the famous author of the four books of Gulliver's Travels, in which the hero, Lemuel Gulliver, embarks on a voyage but gets waylaid and ends up in a fictitious land. In the first book, he arrives in Lilliput, where he awakens to find himself the prisoner of the tiny Lilliputians. Due to its satirical content, this masterpiece was originally published anonymously. A worldwide bestseller since its first publication, *Gulliver's Travels* has never been out of print.

For further details about Swift and his involvement in Northern Ireland, see p. 152.

JEWISH BURIAL GROUND

*Beautiful Jewish burial ground accessible
by appointment only*

79 Church Road, Glengormley, Newtownabbey BT36 6DJ
By appointment only. Contact Rabbi David Singer on: 028 90 775013
Buses: 1a, 1c, 1d, 2a, 13

Accessible by appointment only, the grandiose tombs of Carnmoney Jewish Cemetery are visible from the road, with picturesque views of Belfast Harbour, Cave Hill and Belfast Castle in the distance. On your right as you enter the cemetery, you will see a *tahara* (prayer hall) that is used for funeral services. To the left of the entrance is a spartan plot, marked only by a single plaque denoting it as an infant burial ground.

In a melancholic and romantic atmosphere, the gravestones that fill the cemetery tell the story of the city's Jews and their active participation in Belfast society. They also tell of their roles in the two World Wars and their suffering during the Holocaust. Leslie Leopold, head of the Jewish Burial Society, shows visitors around the graves and recounts touching, insightful and sometimes even amusing anecdotes about the many characters buried here. This beautifully maintained site contains 400 graves, including that of the only Jewish person killed during the Northern Irish conflict. Other notable graves include those of Holocaust survivor

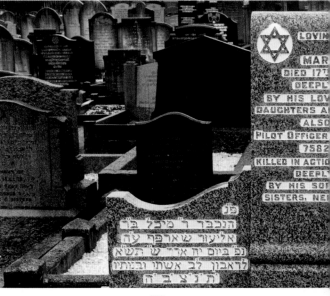

Peter Aubrey, war hero Captain Harold Smith, and four pilots killed while on active service. The cemetery was established at the beginning of the 20th century as Belfast's Jewish community expanded. Prior to that, a specific part of Belfast City Cemetery was dedicated to those of the Jewish faith (see below). Much of the Jewish population at the time lived in the north of the city, so it was thought best to acquire a burial ground here. Carnmoney was chosen after Samuel Freeman and Maurice Goldring purchased 1.6 hectares of land in 1909–10. Sir Otto Jaffe (twice Lord Mayor of Belfast at the turn of the century: see p. 13) joined them as a trustee. The first burials are recorded here in 1913 and the site remains the main Jewish graveyard for Northern Ireland.

A melancholy feeling engulfs you as you wander through the other Jewish burial ground within the City Cemetery on the Falls Road in West Belfast. Here the gravestones have been left to the elements and the site neglected. Despite this, the Jaffe Memorial obelisk is here, which commemorates the contribution of the Jaffe family to Belfast life. If you can find the original bricked-up entrance to these graves, see if you can spot the wording on the lintel above the door. It is a Hebrew inscription, "*Bet Hayim*", which means "House of Life". The gate is padlocked at all times, so it's best to call ahead and check that someone can let you in.

MODEL OF THE MAYFLY

Lilian Bland: Ireland's first female aviator

Lilian Bland Community Park, Ballyclare Rd, Glengormley BT36 5EX
http://www.lilianbland.ie/mayfly/lilian-bland-park/
Buses: 1a, 1b, 1c, 1d, 1e, 1f

In Glengormley Park in Newtownabbey, now renamed the Lilian Bland Community Park, a life-size stainless steel model of a biplane called the *Mayfly* was erected here in 2011 to celebrate the centenary of Lilian Bland's achievements.

The "flying feminist", as she's known, was by all accounts quite an adventure-seeking maverick.

In 1900 she was wearing trousers, smoking openly, drinking alcohol and swearing to boot, all somewhat unconventional pursuits for women at this time. She was also a sports journalist, a keen photographer and a good shot.

In early 1910, Bland was excited and inspired by French aviator Louis Blériot, who had successfully undertaken the first flight across the English Channel.

Eager to demonstrate that flying was not just for men, she began researching the work of the Wright brothers and set about constructing her own homemade biplane glider.

The following year, after collecting an engine from England, she managed to fly the plane on Carnmoney Hill on the outskirts of Belfast, with the assistance of her gardener.

Initially, there was no petrol tank and being too impatient to wait for its arrival, Bland attempted to fashion one out of an empty whisky bottle and her deaf aunt's ear trumpet, down which she poured the fuel. Against all odds, the plane actually flew about 30 metres.

Bland had to wait a while before the plane was ready for her first official flight and then it only hopped some 10 metres or so. However, it was enough to secure her place as the first woman to fly in Ireland.

Her father didn't approve of these "unladylike" activities and persuaded her to take up his offer of a car in return for giving up flying. She duly obliged, and became Ford's first agent in the north of Ireland.

Lilian Bland was born in Kent, England, in 1878. In 1900, following the death of her mother, she went with her widowed father to his native Carnmoney and grew up in Tobercorran House. There is a plaque in her memory at her former dwelling on Glebe Road West, where she grew up. Following her aviation exploits in 1911, she married a cousin, Charles Loftus Bland, and went to live with him at Vancouver Island in Canada. After many years, she returned to England and settled in Cornwall, where she died in the early 1970s, aged 93.

A 19th-century farmhouse, giving a rare insight into rural family life in Victorian times

40 Ballycraigy Road, Newtownabbey BT36 4SX
028 90 832363
www.sentryhill.net
April–September (daily) 2pm–5pm; July and August 10.30am–5.30pm (closed on Mon)
By car: 30 mins from Belfast (M2, M5)

A different world awaits you as you turn down the long and winding tree-lined lane to Sentry Hill Historic House. Away from the noise of the adjacent motorway and housing developments, Sentry Hill offers an escape to a peaceful refuge. Set in 8 hectares of farmland, it is a typical 19th-century farmhouse, although its contents distinguish it from any other buildings of the period. On arrival, one of the first things you notice is the standing stone, possibly dating back to the Bronze Age. Inside, the museum is home to many unusual and interesting objects, from a rare jug commemorating the fall of the Bastille in Paris in 1789 to a stuffed

armadillo. However, as guide Wesley Bonar points out, "Often it's not the object that is of interest, but the story behind it." He believes this is what makes the Sentry Hill collection unique: most objects have a neatly written label penned by former owner, William Fee McKinney, giving details of the item and its history. McKinney was a passionate collector and some of his favourite curiosities are on show: a pike used at the Battle of Antrim during the 1798 Rebellion, a stuffed duck-billed platypus, and McKinney's polished axe heads which were uncovered in New Zealand.

The McKinney family's arrival in this part of the world began with the Jacobite uprising in Scotland in 1715. Generations lived at Sentry Hill, through the 1798 Rebellion, when McKinney's great uncle was killed at the Battle of Antrim, to the First World War, which saw Tom McKinney perish in the Battle of the Somme in 1916. His death is commemorated with a plaque and an oak tree on the front lawn. Sentry Hill House and its farm remained in family ownership until as recently as 1996, with the death of Dr Joe Dundee (b. 1906), grandson of William Fee McKinney. While the exteriors and the house itself have been conserved, the outbuildings have been carefully adapted to offer a variety of facilities for visitors, including an exhibition space, reception, tea room, and resource and education rooms.

PATTERSON'S SPADE MILL

25

The last working water-driven spade mill in daily use in the British Isles

751 Antrim Road, Templepatrick, County Antrim BT39 0AP
028 94 433619
www.nationaltrust.org.uk/pattersons-spade-mill
Every weekend and Bank Holiday in April, May and September: 12pm–4pm
(last tour 3pm)
June, July and August: Sat–Wed 12pm–4pm
Bus services from Belfast to Cookstown: bus stops at gates
By road: on Antrim to Belfast road, A6; M2 exit 4
The site itself could present difficulties for people with mobility issues. Contact the mill to check access

Founded in 1917, Patterson's Spade Mill is a small but fascinating workshop that welcomes visitors who are keen to gain an insight into the manufacturing of spades of all shapes and sizes. It is also the last working water-driven spade mill in daily use in the British Isles.

The spade is an important cultural emblem for Northern Ireland as it represents the high value placed on agricultural life across the province. Before 1750, most spades in Ireland were made by blacksmiths, but by the early to mid-19th century, they were produced in specialised mills.

Today, Patterson's Spade Mill still uses techniques which go back to the Industrial Revolution: full working mechanisms are still in opera-

©*National Trust / Cliff Mason*

tion, allowing visitors to gain an idea of some of the working conditions during the 19th century. You will find many blasts from the past here and be exposed to the grit and grime of a workplace where the noise of industry permeates the air.

You can listen to the hammers at work and feel the heat as red-hot billets of steel are removed from the forge and fashioned into spades using the mill's massive trip hammer.

You can also witness the key skills in the art of spade making, mastered over decades and kept alive in Patterson's. In the past, during full production, the mill would have produced an average of one spade per man per hour.

By the end of your visit, you will have seen all the stages of spade production: the shoulders of the spade are forged first, then a spike is pressed down into the white-hot metal to open the slot where the handle will eventually fit.

This hole is then filled with ash and closed up while the spade's blade is "forged out", before being reopened at the end to form a recognisable and usable spade.

©*National Trust / John Millar*

Handcrafted spades are on sale and made to specification for special occasions. A quality, forged spade will set you back £125. Pretty good value considering the work involved.

26

TEMPLETOWN MAUSOLEUM

Georgian-style mausoleum in a tiny graveyard

Antrim Rd, Templepatrick BT39 0AH
11am–6pm every day
Buses: 110, 120, 253, 571, 573 (Ulsterbus); and Airport Express 300
By car: A6 Antrim Road

The elegant Templetown Mausoleum is the jewel in the crown and the dominating feature of the tiny graveyard situated within the grounds of Castle Upton.

Although the castle remains private property, the graveyard is under National Trust care and open to the public.

The graveyard is over three centuries old and although most headstones are well maintained, some are in a state of disrepair. Renowned Scottish architect Robert Adam designed this Grade

A listed mausoleum in the 1780s for the Rt Hon. Arthur Upton. It is a fine example of Georgian neoclassical style with a majestic triumphal arch, decorated with classical urns and circular leafy reliefs.

You will probably find the entrance open, so take a peek inside at the tombs of Castle Upton's high-profile residents from centuries ago. The inscriptions are on marble tablets and include various barons, viscounts, colonels and knights.

The Stone Chapel of St Patrick supposedly stood roughly where the

mausoleum stands today. St Patrick is said to have baptised locals on this spot in the fifth century, using the local Holy Well.

Folklore has it that the well dried up when people began blasting for a quarry and desecrating the chapel a century ago. It is believed by some that their actions angered the faeries, or "little people".

Robert Adam (1728–92) was one of Scotland's most revered architects and came from a wealthy family. His father was also an architect. He was lucky enough to spend five years abroad studying classical buildings and ancient Roman sites in Italy and France. When he returned to London in 1758, he set up an architecture practice with his brother. Using what he had seen and experienced abroad, he created his own "Adam" style, characterised by a lightness and freedom in the way he used classical elements. He was considered far more daring than his predecessors, which secured his reputation far and wide.

Notice a small opening built into the wall of the cemetery at its entrance. This was a donation box for the graveyard keeper, perhaps to encourage him to keep the gravestones neat and the grass cut. The door to the box has long since disappeared.

27

HOLESTONE

Visit an ancient lovestone and find eternal love and happiness

24 Holestone Road, Doagh, Ballyclare BT39 0TJ
Bus: 153 from the Europa Bus Centre
By car: approx. 20/25 minutes from Belfast city centre

If you're on the hunt for eternal love and happiness, try visiting the mysterious holestone (also called lovestone) with your intended. An ancient Celtic rock dating from the Bronze Age and standing at just under 1.5 metres tall, the stone can be found atop a grassy outcrop on a hill a couple of kilometres north-west of the village of Doagh. From here, you can enjoy sweeping views across the Six Mile Water.

The smooth hole is at waist height and funnel-shaped, petering down to only 10 cm in diameter at one end. Why it was created, and what its purpose was, is the subject of myth and legend.

During the 18th century, however, it acquired a reputation as a place where couples came to exchange vows and pledge eternal love to one another. A woman's hand can usually pass through and hold the hand of her beloved on the other side. It's too narrow for most men's hands to pass through.

It is thought that rural communities took to using the holestone for matrimonial ceremonies as clergy were not always available to carry out such services at convenient times, so locals had to take matters into their own hands. It would have been a good enough option to save women from the stigma of giving birth outside wedlock, and they could always get their marriage ratified by a priest at a later date.

According to a plaque at the site, betrothals at the stone date back to the 1830s. Contemporary documents describe the neighbourhood around the stone as rather insalubrious: "a cesspit full of filthy shacks housing farm workers". It was said that the shacks were full of prostitutes and illegitimate children and the residents were generally "dirty, drunken, slovenish and idle".

Ultimately, the dioceses of Down and Connor became separated when the then Bishop decided he wanted nothing to do with the people of Connor, whom he, too, described as being more like beasts than men. But today all this is forgotten as couples still visit the stone to renew their vows, or pledge undying love to one another, ensuring the enigma of the stone persists.

Stones perforated in the same manner as the holestone are common in Ireland and are often seen in burial grounds attached to extremely ancient churches. Some are inscribed with ancient Ogham characters, which were in use in Ireland between the 3rd and 6th centuries, prior to the introduction of Christianity.

POGUE'S ENTRY HISTORICAL COTTAGE

28

The rags-to-riches story of one of Northern Ireland's most prolific authors

Church Street, Antrim, County Antrim BT41 4BA
028 94 428331
June–Sept: Thurs and Fri 2pm–5pm, Sat 10am–1pm and 2pm–5pm
Other times by appointment
Free
Buses: 108a, 109, 109a, 109b, 109c
By train to Antrim train station

Open to the public following renovation in the 1960s, in a historic corner of Antrim, sits the childhood home of the best-selling 19th-century author, missionary and social reformer, Alexander Irvine. This gem of a cottage is often overlooked but is well worth a visit to see how an Irish family lived in the mid-1800s.

Known as "Pogue's Entry", the cottage stands just off the road in the centre of town and has a peaceful garden, surrounded by period buildings.

The mud floors and stone walls give us a glimpse of what life would have been like here in Irvine's time, and the rooms contain books and documents, as well as teapots and other utensils. Alexander Irvine was born

into poverty in 1863. His father, Jamie, was a shoemaker and although his mother Anna was educated, her love for Jamie led her to stray from her former life as a devotee of the Church. Indeed, she left her comfortable Crumlin home to be with him and lived a life of great hardship. Alexander was the ninth of their twelve children. He emigrated to the United States in 1888 – famously with just one dollar in his pocket – and undertook a variety of jobs such as lift attendant, porter, milk-cart driver and salesman. By 1890, he had begun to work as a missionary among people living in deprivation in the Bowery area of New York. He joined the Socialist Party in 1903 and graduated in theology from Yale University.

Cottage guide Bill McBride really brings the visit to life for visitors. "Irvine left Ireland completely illiterate," he explains, "and within six years of serving in the Royal Marines he had become educated, fully literate in English and fluent in five or more languages." Irvine received a gallantry medal for his services with General Gordon in Khartoum and eventually became pastor of the Church of the Ascension on New York's Fifth Avenue. His book, *My Lady of The Chimney Corner* (1913), recalls his boyhood years in Pogue's Entry and describes the lives of Irish peasants during the post-famine days. He is also remembered for *The Souls of Poor Folk* (1921). Irvine died in California in 1941. His ashes were returned to Northern Ireland in 1944, to be buried beside his parents in an Antrim cemetery. An Ulster History Circle Blue Plaque has been erected there, commemorating this great Ulsterman.

Belfast City Library houses a collection of typescripts, photos and postcards that provide a fascinating insight into the life of Alexander Irving. It includes documents pertaining to a 1921 visit to see the Prime Minister, David Lloyd George, at 10 Downing Street in London.

WITCH'S STONE AT THE ROUND TOWER

A mysterious stone

Steeple Road, Antrim BT41 1BL
Buses: 1a, 1c, 1d, 1e, 1f, 1g

I n the area known locally as "The Steeple", the imposing 28-metre-high round tower is one of the best-preserved of its type in the whole of Ireland. Dated to the 10th or 11th century, the tower is all that remains of the once famous monastery of Antrim.

The monastery was reputedly founded by St Aedh in 495 and destroyed circa 1018, although no one knows for sure. This round tower

was probably built to the west of the west door of the monastic church.

To the left of the tower, the stone that seems at first glance rather unremarkable is in fact a *bulláun*: a large stone with sizeable hollows in it, typically found at religious sites (see p. 61).

Legend has it that the hollows were created by a witch who, dismayed by the Christian monks building the tower, climbed to the top and flung herself off. She is said to have landed on the stone beneath and formed the hollows with her elbows and knees.

A sign at the site states that the witch must have glided part of the way as the stone is some distance from the tower …

This stone has intrigued locals over the years because the larger of its hollows seems to continuously fill up with water. Oddly, this has been the case even in times of drought. Over the years, the stone has often been used to baptise infants. Monks also used it to prepare food and mix herbs.

NEARBY

Antrim Castle Gardens, located at Randalstown Road, BT41 4LQ, are not to be missed: see next page.

THE STONE OF ANTRIM CASTLE GARDENS

Where Viscount Massereene died while doing a spot of gardening

Randalstown Road, County Antrim BT41 4LH
028 94 481338
www.antrimandnewtownabbey.gov.uk
Mon, Wed and Fri 9.30am–5pm, Tues and Thurs 9.30am–9.30pm, Sat and Sun 10am–5pm
Free entry to the gardens
Buses: 80a, 80b, 80c, 80h
By car: outside Antrim town centre, off A26 on A6

There are a number of intriguing details to be seen at the Antrim Castle Gardens once you get close to what is known as the Walled Pleasure Garden: a special stone is located where the lower and upper levels meet at the bottom of the garden, among the ruins of the stone wall. Look for two stones attached to the wall and stacked on top of each other.

Once you've located what looks like an unusual stone step, search for some metal carvings of a name engraved upon it. This marks the spot where 10th Viscount Massereene tragically died while pulling up a weed in 1863. He had lovingly planted the garden for his wife Olivia, and

had the nearby tunnels excavated so that Lady Massereene could walk through the grounds in privacy, without having to battle the elements.

The gardens at Antrim Castle (formerly Massereene Castle) include arbours, tunnels, winding paths, artificial mounds and tree roots capped with antlers.

All that remains of Antrim Castle is a slightly raised grassy mound. The castle was built on the banks of the Sixmilewater River in the early 17th century by Englishman Sir Hugh Clotworthy, and added to and expanded over time.

His son John Clotworthy became the 1st Viscount Massereene and enlarged the castle in 1662. It was rebuilt in a Georgian style hundreds of years later, and an octagonal turret was added in 1887. Although the turret is still standing, a fire destroyed the castle in 1922.

The recently renovated grounds are open to the public. They have remained largely intact and much as they were when the Skeffington family began laying them out in the late 17th century.

A small burial ground contains the graves of the Massereene family, notably the 12th Viscount Massereene and his daughter, Lady Diana Skeffington, who died from typhoid aged 21. Another stone slab commemorates the 13th Viscount Massereene, who raced for the Aston Martin team at Le Mans in 1937.

CRANFIELD CHURCH AND WELL

One of the most atmospheric Christian sites in Ireland

Churchtown Point, Cranfield Road, Cranfield
Dawn to dusk
Bus 222 from Belfast Europa bus station to Randalstown. Alight at The Gables bus stop, then take a local taxi to Cranfield Road (approx. 5 mins)

Hidden at the back end of Cranfield Road is an ancient and mystical spot that has been a place of pilgrimage for centuries. The small church here dates from 1306 but the site was probably under monastic care prior to that, as marked on a stone.

As you stand within the original stone walls of the church, you can still see the doorway with its outward pointed arch in the west gable wall and the remains of a tall window where the altar would have been. A large cross rests against the inner wall: it is not the original but a replica of the ancient cross that would have been placed to mark the boundary of church land. When you stand in the tiny yet atmospheric graveyard attached to the church, it feels like a theatre set … although you have to swipe your hand around to deter the numerous insects that thrive here amid undulating mounds and ancient headstones. It is believed that St Olcran, a disciple of St Patrick, lies buried here with soil brought specially from Rome. The oldest visible date on a headstone is 1704. With its association to St Olcran, this graveyard and its nearby well have long been revered as miraculous places. The well is easy to spot within the boundary of a small stone wall. The tree that sits in front of it is draped

with rags of various colours and textures and the odd prayer note. Pilgrims still journey here, particularly for three specific days between May and the end of June each year. According to tradition, this is when the well is most likely to flood, bringing gypsum crystals to the surface that are believed to have healing properties. In former times, pilgrims would collect these gems, using them as prayer aids, or they would swallow them to ensure a safe passage by sea. Sludge and mud now act as a deterrent to visitors attempting to dip fragments of cloth into the previously clean waters. However, some still persevere, believing that as the cloth rots on the tree, their loved one's ailments will disappear.

RAMS ISLAND

The Blytonesque island with a military past

Lough Neagh
Approx. 2 km offshore from Lennymore Bay and Sandy Bay on the eastern shore
To visit, call Michael Savage on 07715 368050
www.ramsisland.org
By car: 40-mins drive from Belfast to Lisburn
On summer weekends, the River Bann & Lough Neagh Association operates a licensed passenger vessel from Sandy Bay on a demand basis
Anyone with their own vessel is welcome to visit all year round. It takes about 10 minutes to cross to the island

Accessed from a small boat called the *Island Warrior*, Rams Island has a 1,000-year-old round tower and the ruins of a 19th-century house, once inhabited by members of the Irish aristocracy.

Lord O'Neill purchased the island for 100 guineas from a local fisherman in 1804, and when he lived here, his parties attracted the great and the good of Belfast and beyond.

A caretaker family, the Cardwells, managed the property from the 1920s and became well known in their own right.

Stories of Jane Cardwell, its tenant caretaker and champion gardener, abound: she lived here until she was 99.

Considered the "Queen of the Island", she lived off the land with her menagerie of animals and home-grown fruit and veg. Following her

death, the island was largely neglected, but in recent years it has found a new lease of life.

It is currently looked after by the River Bann & Lough Neagh Association, a group of 50- 60 volunteers who have helped to regenerate the island and attract new visitors.

Most people come here on day-trips as camping on the island is only permitted with prior permission, and is completely forbidden during the birds' nesting season from March to June. Aside from its importance as a "party island" in O'Neill's heyday, Rams Island has great historic value. Its monastic round tower, 13-metres-high, stands at the top of a steep hill near the east shore. In the early nineteenth century, O'Neill built a charming thatched cottage just below the tower, but it was destroyed by vandals in the late 1940s.

The island played an important role during the Second World War, when a number of Belgian and American servicemen trained here. The island's beech trees bear witness to their presence: the men carved their names, home states and the year (1944) onto the bark.

Volunteer Michael Savage, who dredges the lake here, says he often digs up wartime relics, including cartridges used in training exercises. Many are marked as having been made in the United States in 1943.

ALPHABETICAL INDEX

ACKNOWLEDGEMENTS:

WITH THANKS TO:

Colin Agnew, Joyce Anderson, Michelle Ashmore, Stuart Bailey, Sam Baird, Jean Barber, Rev. Chris Bennett, William Blair, Wesley Bonar, Derek Booker, Nicola Gordon Bowe, Jim Bradley, Larry Breen, Leanne Briggs, Christopher Burns, Fiona Byrne, Heather Chesney, Rev. Vernon Clegg, Anne Cleland, Fionnualla Coiste, Joy Conkey, Edna Cooper, Ernie Cromie, Janice Crow, Peter and Dympna Curran, Samantha Curry, Colin Dawson, Rita Duffy, Brighdin Farren, Bobby Foster, Richard Gaston, Gavin Glass, Jana Gough, Tom Hartley, Dr Stanley Hawkins, Susan Hickey, Lesley Holmes, Catherine Hunter, Sam and Paul Hunter, Chris Ibbotson, Alex Irvine, Brendan Jamison, Daniel Jewesbury, Francis Keenan, Martin Keery, Eugene Kelly, Sarah Kelly, Marian Kelso, Mark Kennedy, John Kindness, Rev. Jack Lamb, Lesley Leopold, Zoe Lindsay, Samantha Livingstone, Derek Lockwood, Dr Orla Lowry, Suzanne Lyle, Jonathan Madison, Winnie Magee, Toni Maguire, Norman McBride, William McBride, Alistair Mc Cann, Paul Mc Cann, Mc Carron Family, Linda Mc Cullough, Eva Mc Dermott, Kevin Mc Donald, Brian Mc Kee, Patrick Mc Lain, Cathryn Mc Oscar, Seamus Milliken, Elizabeth Milroy, Jim Moore, Catherine Morrow, Jason Mulligan, Sherrin Murphy, Sharon Mushtaq, Amberlea Neely, Jim and Josephine O'Hagan, Eugene O'Neill, Ryan O'Neill, Raymond O'Regan, Dr Desie O'Reilly, Conor Owen, Colin Patterson, Vivienne Pollock, Neil Porteous, Katy Radford, Brad Robson, Jenny Russell, Michael Savage, Rev. Andy Scott, Fr. Michael Sheehan, Holly Sinclair, Gavin Sloan, Rabbi David Singer, Lyndsy Spence, Roy Spence, Susan Taggart, Vincent Taggart, Rev Dr Livingstone Thompson, Viv Timmins, Lauren Turner, Mimi Turtle, Louise Walsh, Graham Walton, Jerry Ward, Margaret Ward, Rachel Wetherall, Eleanor Wheeler, Karen White, Ross Wilson, Petra Wolsley, Claire Woods, Sarah Ziman.

With special thanks to David Donnelly at the Radisson Blu Hotel, Belfast who showed such generosity towards the authors during the research stages of this Secret Belfast guide.

PHOTO CREDITS:

Gavin Sloan Photography
https://www.gavinsloanphotography.co.uk/
Pages: 10, 12, 14-15, 16, 18, 24-5, 26-7, 30-31, 34-35, 36-37, 38, 44-45, 48-49, 50-51, 52-53, 54-55, 60-61, 62-63, 64-65, 68-69, 72-73, 76,77, 78-79, 80-81, 86-87, 88, 92-93, 94-95, 96-97, 98-99, 104-105, 112-113, 116, 118-119, 120-121, 132-133, 136-137, 138-139, 160-161, 162-163, 164-165, 170, 172-173, 176-177, 184-185, 186-187

Hunters Brothers Photography
Cover image: Botanic Gardens, Belfast.
Pages: 32-33, 66-67, 70-71, 74-75, 82-3, 100-101, 106-107, 110-111, 114-115, 122-123, 158-159, 166, 168-169, 178-179

Vincent Taggart
Pages: 148-149, 152-3, 156-157

Official Thanks
58-59 Jason Mulligan
102-3 Alistair Mc Cann
108-109 Heather Chesney East Belfast Partnership
117 Mimi Turtle
126-131 Leanne Briggs, Alex Irvine at the North Ards Museum
134-135 DeLorean Car, Photograph @National Museums Northern Ireland. Collection Ulster Folk and Transport Museum.
140-141 Flame Gas Works
142-143 - Andrew Jackson Cottage
144 Seamus Milliken
150-151 Zoe Lindsay at Mid and East Antrim Borough Council
174-175 ©National Trust / Cliff Mason
180-181 Antrim and Newtonabbey Borough Council
183 Lynsey Spence
188-189 Michael Savage

Maps: **Louisa Keyworth** - Layout design: **Coralie Cintrat** - Layout: **Iperbole** - Proofreading: **Jana Gough** - Edition: **Clémence Mathé**

© JONGLEZ 2018
Registration of copyright: May 2018 – Edition: 01
ISBN: 978-2-36195-263-1
Printed in Bulgaria by Dedrax